D1806374

EX LIBRIS

ELWAY

THE BOOK OF THAME

FRONT COVER: Stukeley's View of Thame, 1724. (MN)

ABOVE: The Market Place in 1868. From an etching by H. Hinton. (BL)
BELOW: An early 19th century drawing of the High Street. (BL)

THE BOOK OF THAME

BY

GERALD CLARKE

BARRACUDA BOOKS LIMITED
BUCKINGHAM, ENGLAND
MCMLXXVIII

PUBLISHED BY BARRACUDA BOOKS LIMITED
BUCKINGHAM, ENGLAND
AND PRINTED BY
BOWMAN-ROCASTLE LIMITED
HERTFORD, ENGLAND

BOUND BY
BOOKBINDERS OF LONDON LIMITED
LONDON N5

JACKET PRINTED BY
WHITE CRESCENT PRESS LIMITED LUTON, ENGLAND

LITHOGRAPHY BY
SOUTH MIDLANDS LITHOPLATES LIMITED
LUTON, ENGLAND

DISPLAY TYPE SET IN
MONOTYPE BASKERVILLE SERIES 169
BY SOUTH BUCKS TYPESETTERS LIMITED
BEACONSFIELD, ENGLAND

TEXT SET IN 12/14PT BASKERVILLE
BY BEAVER REPROGRAPHICS LIMITED
BUSHEY, ENGLAND

© GERALD CLARKE 1978

All rights reserved. No part of this publication may be reproduced,
stored in a retrieval system, or transmitted, in any form or by any
means, electronic, mechanical, photocopying, recording or
otherwise without the prior permission of Barracuda Books Limited.

Any copy of this book issued by the Publisher as clothbound or as a
paperback is sold subject to the condition that it shall not by way of
trade or otherwise, be lent, re-sold, hired out or otherwise circulated
without the Publisher's prior consent, in any form of binding or
cover other than that in which it is published, and without a similar
condition including this condition being imposed on a
subsequent purchaser.

ISBN 0 86023 053 8

Contents

Introduction and Acknowledgements

This is by no means the first History of Thame; at least four other authors have essayed the same area, and formal credit must first be paid to these works. Lupton's book, written in the 1860s, is itself history now, though unfortunately many of its statements cannot be verified. Lee's massive volume is a most scholarly work, as are his extensive working notes and files in the Bodleian Library. More recently, William Guest and J. Howard Brown produced their *History of Thame*, and the *Victoria County History of Oxfordshire* on Thame has appeared. This book owes a great debt to these works, and I have not hesitated to draw extensively from them.

In common with previous historians of the town, I have faced several problems. The first is simply geographical: 'Thame' has been construed as 'The Thame area' for the earliest parts, but I have limited myself very much to the town for the later chapters. Whole histories could be written about the surrounding villages and hamlets! Secondly, tracing visual material has not always been easy. Thame, with its position on the boundary, has tended to miss out on the major collections in the County. This has meant that the picture collection has had to concentrate on views and buildings rather than artefacts.

For help in the preparation of material for this book, I am indebted to Norman Lilley and Norman Waters for photographic work; John Seabrook for preparing the diagrams and maps; Gerald Southern of the Thame Historical Society for help, and access to a large number of photographs; and W. Mackenzie, Michael Newitt and Philip Smith for the loan of photographs and pictures: Messrs Mott and R. Baylis and I. Shrimpton for help with material, and Mrs. Jean Pettit for helping type the script.

Thanks are due to Oxfordshire County Libraries, especially the staff of Thame Library, and to Peter Kingham of Kinghams, Buttermarket, Thame, for help with the essential subscription list facility.

Formal acknowledgements are due to the following for permission to reproduce copyright material: The Bodleian Library, Oxford; Miss S. Barnes, County Archivist, and the County Record Office, Oxford; The Aylesbury Museum; The Ashmolean Museum, Oxford; The Public Record Office (Crown Copyright Reserved); Oxfordshire Museum Services, Woodstock; British Oxygen Company Ltd; The Department of Aerial Photography, University of Cambridge.

Finally, thanks should go to local newspapers and Thame Radio for continued interest (and publicity!); to all the people in Thame who have helped or loaned material; and lastly to the Publisher, Clive Birch, for support and advice all through the project.

Brill, 25th October 1978

Foreword

Many ancient houses have survived in Thame, thanks to the gentle pace of Victorian progress in the locality. Thanks to the inheritance of an exceptionally wide street Thame's rulers have not been led into the temptation of wholesale official vandalism to which so many post-war councils succumbed—though its beautiful ancient grammar school building was shamefully demolished.

The splendid monument in the Church to Lord Williams at Thame commemorates the founder of that school. It keeps his name and educated some of the greatest men in 17th century law, politics, religion, academic life and local history. Williams himself 'served conscientiously under four contrasting regimes, one of a core of loyal administrators.' He could dissolve monasteries or burn the protestant Archbishop Cranmer with impartial zeal for official policy; yet his school produced in the great local landlord and parliamentary leader, Hampden, a hero who died in Thame of a wound received fighting for his principles before his party triumphed and power tarnished its reputation. It was a time when our district was a No-Man's land east of Charles I's capital, Oxford.

Any book that helps nourish a feeling for the past will contribute to a more appreciative present and so to a richer future.

W. O. Hassall

Grysilde the Second

From thense wheare hee came, faste iumpe by his syde,
Accompayned hym the lady *Anne Bullayne*,
All pleasaunte, fresche and gallaunt that tyde,
Good *Grysilde* following, as one of her trayne,
At whiche manye (that wise weare) did disdayne
So noble a woman to bee forsake,
And in her steade so meane a thing to take.

For thorowe *Thame*, that gentle Market Towne,
The Kynge then issued vpp to *London*warde,
Where dyverse and many their headys henge downe
To see the case with *Grysilde*, how it fared,
Unto their hartys God wote, it went full harde,
And thus did say mutteringe as they stoode still—
" Christe saue good *Grysilde* to His blessed will."

William Forrest c1551

9

Preface

Visitors to Thame often comment on its picturesqueness, a quality which the inhabitants also intermittently notice, admire, and do their best to protect and enhance. But it is a picturesqueness that derives far more from the town's history than from any recent and deliberate attempt, either by public authority or by private inhabitants, to preserve its visual character. Not only historians but also everyone interested in the appearance of Thame will be grateful to Mr Clarke for writing this book.

Nowadays, Thame is within easy access of Oxford and Aylesbury, High Wycombe and Henley, Harwell and Bicester, London and the industrial Midlands — it even appears to be on a direct route for heavy vehicles from the Continent to South Wales. One aspect of the town's history that Mr Clarke brings out well is that, unlike today, for most of its thousand or fifteen hundred years Thame has led an isolated existence as one of those numerous minor and almost self-sufficient communities of which, at least until the Industrial Revolution, England was constituted. Of course in varying degrees they all came under the same national political, economic, social and religious influences, and they underwent common developments, but in the end each community proves a unique organism. That is what makes the study of a town both an historically important and a pleasurable activity; Mr Clarke's book is consequently a significant work as well as being thoroughly enjoyable.

Frank Jessup

Air view of Central Thame.

ABOVE: Prehistoric elephant bones from the Thame area. (AM) BELOW: Saxon urns from the grounds of Tythrop House, near Thame. (AM)

In The Beginning

Writing the story of earliest Thame is like trying to picture the whole of a completed puzzle from only two or three pieces. For its earliest history, one can only make guesses. If dinosaurs once patrolled the area, they were not considerate enough to deposit their mortal remains systematically. There are, however, some bones of deer, oxen, horses and elephant from the area in the Aylesbury and Natural History Museums, the sole surviving remains of the extensive life which must have originally populated this area. Fossils are regularly found in the chalk of the Chilterns which help eke out our knowledge of this earliest period, and thus geology plays a major part in reconstructing our earliest picture from the past.

Thame lies in a clay area, bounded by limestone to the North and South. Originally, the area would have been heavily afforested. The site of Thame itself is on a ridge, above the River Thame, and it is the river which gave the town its name, thought to mean either 'dark' or 'spreading water'—descriptions which still apply yearly when the river floods the water meadows which border its meandering course.

To such an area was primitive man attracted, and recent evidence suggests that he came in considerably larger numbers than was at one time suspected. Thame itself has yielded a few remains—a Neolithic flint-axe and pottery (both found in local fields, though the exact location of these finds is now uncertain), and, more recently, evidence of an 'occupation site' adjacent to the railway line and the BOC factory, which yielded Late Iron Age pottery and some signs of pits and ditches. The site obviously continued in use for some time, for Romano-British wares were found *in situ*. Some human remains and items of copper were also uncovered. To this list one must add Iron Age coins inscribed ANDOCO and BODVOC found locally, and a Belgic Jar dug up recently by a badger.

If one extends this list by including the rather more extensive finds from Tythrop (only two miles down the Risborough road, though just over the County Border) and the M40 excavations, it becomes clear that there were established and quite permanent settlements in this area over 2,000 years ago.

The area seems to have been a contested one from the start, a frontier between the Catuvellauni and the Dodunni tribes in Saxon times. When the conquering Romans arrived in 43 AD, they subdued the warring tribes and brought a modicum of peace, but there is not much evidence of systematic Roman settlement in Thame.

To the Romano-British pottery mentioned above has to be added three Roman coins found in Thame, and a Roman cemetery and coins at Long Crendon, all discovered in the last century. However, the nearest Roman road, running from Dorchester to Alcester, is quite distant from Thame, although the Icknield Way over the Chilterns was probably in use during this time. On balance, the case for an established Roman settlement in Thame has yet to be proven.

The departure of the Romans from Britain in the fourth century AD left a confused vacuum, into which sundry Germanic tribes gradually infiltrated. The scanty evidence available suggests that they had reached the area by the 6th century, taking AEylesburh (i.e. Aylesbury) in 571. From then on, the area became a frontier again, this time between the rival kingdoms of Wessex and Mercia. It was during this period that the first written mention of Thame occurred, for according to a Saxon charter, King Wulfhere of Mercia is said to have 'subscribed the sign of the cross' in Thame in 675 AD. Saxon urns discovered at Tythrop add weight to the suggestion of settlement in the area and certainly, the Saxons colonised South Oxfordshire, and from 635 a Bishopric seems to have existed at Dorchester, and Thame's development was to be tied to this event, so the town had probably grown as a burgh, or settlement, in Saxon times.

In 971, the *Anglo-Saxon Chronicle* records that Archbishop Oskytel (who was Suffragen Bishop of Dorchester and Archbishop of York) died at Thame. From the context, it is clear that he had some kind of domicile here, probably in Thame Park. Thus the Bishops of Dorchester had become landowners in Thame, and when the see was transferred to Lincoln in about 1078, the ecclesiastical link remained. But by then, new masters had arrived and were at the helm of Britain: the Normans were here.

The Normans imposed their own system of control on this newly conquered territory. For Thame, this meant the introduction of feudalism and the Manorial system. The Domesday Book records that Remigius, Bishop of Dorchester, held the Manor of Thame. In return for the land granted to him by the King, he had to provide five knights for royal use, should the need arise. Apart from these knights, Domesday Book mentions 27 villeins, 26 borders and five slaves in Thame. A mill, probably powered by water and situated on the river, is also mentioned.

The Manor was sold in 1547 by Henry Holbeach, Bishop of Lincoln, to the Protector Somerset, who in turn passed it on to Sir John Williams. From then on, the title passed through the Berties, Earls of Abingdon. However, it seems that Old and New Thame were regarded as separate Manors, as were Priestend and North Weston. The complicated lineage of these (and lesser) manors can be pursued further in the *Victoria County History of Oxfordshire*, Volume 6, and therefore needs no duplication here.

Overhead view of the British Oxygen Site, where many finds have been
made. A barrow is visible in the field above.

15

Romano-British pottery from the BOC site.

ABOVE LEFT: A coin, dating from the 1st Century AD, showing Pegasus (?), found in Thame.   RIGHT: A Saxon brooch found locally, (AM) and BELOW: the world of archaeological conjecture: a possible site of a hill fort ¾ mile ENE from Thame.   The aerial photograph shows soil marks which possibly represent a rectangle of ditches. (UCDAP)

Overhead view of central Thame, showing the Burgage tenements, and the
large space provided for the markets.

The Market Town

Mediaeval Thame consisted of three distinct parts—Old Thame, centred around the Church, and possibly dating back to the 7th Century AD, New Thame, which grew up in the 12th and 13th Centuries, comprising the broad centre of the town and Priestend, which had its own field system, probably associated with the ownership of the Prebendal.

Little apart from the Church remains of the early settlement, but the New Town laid out from 1221 was of a distinctive pattern, and the shape of the present town centre still corresponds with the mediaeval layout. The Bishop of Lincoln was first granted permission in 1215 to establish fairs and markets in his manorial possessions, and Thame's market was established in 1227—hence the wide span of High Street, reputed to be the second widest in the country.

At about the same time, burgages or long strips of land branching off the High Street were established. There were 76 in 1305, though some seem to have been divided up even at that early stage. The burgages most probably contained shops (there is record of 18 shops erected from 1251 onwards 'in the Market of Thame in the King's highway, to the harm of the Royal dignity'), but merchants also seem to have owned some. The characteristic length of these holdings can still be seen most clearly between High Street and Southern Road. These developments established Thame as a town.

The main Oxford to Aylesbury road was specially diverted to bring travellers into the centre of the new town for the jollifications of market and fair. Its old course, by the vicarage and Lashlake, can still be seen. No doubt some Thame residents of the present day may care to muse that their present tribulations from traffic would be less had the road stayed where it was originally. But the market set Thame up as the focus of the area, and brought moderate prosperity to the town for centuries to come. The Bishop's motives in establishing the market were of course not entirely altruistic; he stood to gain a sizeable sum in the way of tolls, stall fees and fines of unruly attenders, levied at court by his bailiff, not to mention the 'Luke's pence' paid by some merchants as a sweetener to avoid the greater exactions of toll money which could be charged to the unwary.

Thus grew up the apparatus of the Market Town—a market cross (which was unfortunately destroyed in the 16th Century), a Market Hall, in which the courts took place (the earliest known one dated from the 16th Century); and gallows and stocks to complete the picture. The Birdcage Inn was possibly the bridewell or prison, at this time. Paving was installed in the market in 1550 by the churchwardens. Today's Buttermarket and Cornmarket serve to remind us that the market stalls were segregated into areas; other street names, like Cock Row, Sheep Row, Butcher Row and Drapery Row also apparently existed 400 years ago, and Buttermarket was still known as Middle Row in the last century.

It has been calculated that the population of mediaeval Thame may have been in the region of 1,000 (Brown and Guest: *History of Thame*). The vast majority of these, of course, were tenants or vassalls of the Lord of the Manor, and a strict hierarchy existed according to the amount of their land and possessions. They were bound to the Lord by feudal ties, but even in the 14th Century, money rents were being paid by several Thame tenants, a process which was exacerbated in many areas by a series of circumstances centring around the Black Death from 1348 onwards. When labour was in short supply, tenants were able to slip their traditional bonds for wages. The dreaded plague had other long-term effects as well. It annihilated one third of England's population, causing villages and land to be deserted. However, in the Thame area, most deserted villages from the mediaeval period appear to have resulted from enclosure for sheep-farming.

'Your sheep, that were wont to be so meek and tame and so small eaters, now, as I hear say, be become so great devourers, and so wild, that they eat up and swallow down the very men themselves' wrote Sir Thomas More in *Utopia,* and it is in the south Midlands that the wealth and impact of wool may be most clearly seen. The Cistercian monks of Thame Abbey had started the process of enclosure locally by fencing in parts of their estate at Attington in about 1450, and the Wenmans who succeeded them in the 16th Century continued the process. Lord Williams himself left six flocks of sheep in his will. The Dormer family were also involved in the trade, Geoffry (died 1502) being a Merchant of the Staple of Calais. His heir was obviously a man of substance, too, for 'Place House,' his stone mansion in North Street, was chosen as the overnight resting place for Lord Williams's coffin in 1559. The later Dormers owned and built several mansions, and achieved considerable eminence. The Quatremain family also prospered in wool. Previously, the same family had built Rycote Chapel. Appropriately, there is still a wool staple in Thame.

Many crafts flourished in the town in the Middle Ages, and Thame seems to have acquired an especial reputation for glazing. Others, like the Stribblehills, prospered in drink. There were twenty victuallers in the town in 1587, for example. Several mercers seem to have had links with London at this time. As a result of this relative prosperity, New Thame gradually overhauled Old Thame in importance and wealth. In 1327, New Thame had 67 taxpayers, contributing a total of £6 7s 11d, and Old Thame had 50 who paid a total of £5 3s 6d.

The town is fortunate in possessing several examples of timber-framed buildings

20

from the late Middle Ages. These buildings show the prosperity of the mediaeval community. Their survival nowadays is of course assured on picturesque grounds, but paradoxically, they were spared demolition through the previous two centuries only through the relative poverty of the town, as there has never been any large-scale redevelopment of Thame.

Examples of mediaeval timber-framed buildings: two houses and the Birdcage Inn.

LEFT: Mediaeval objects found locally — a sword, brooch and medallion. CENTRE: 12th century seal found in a Thame field. RIGHT: Three old houses in Thame, as drawn by Lee. They are still recognisable.

22

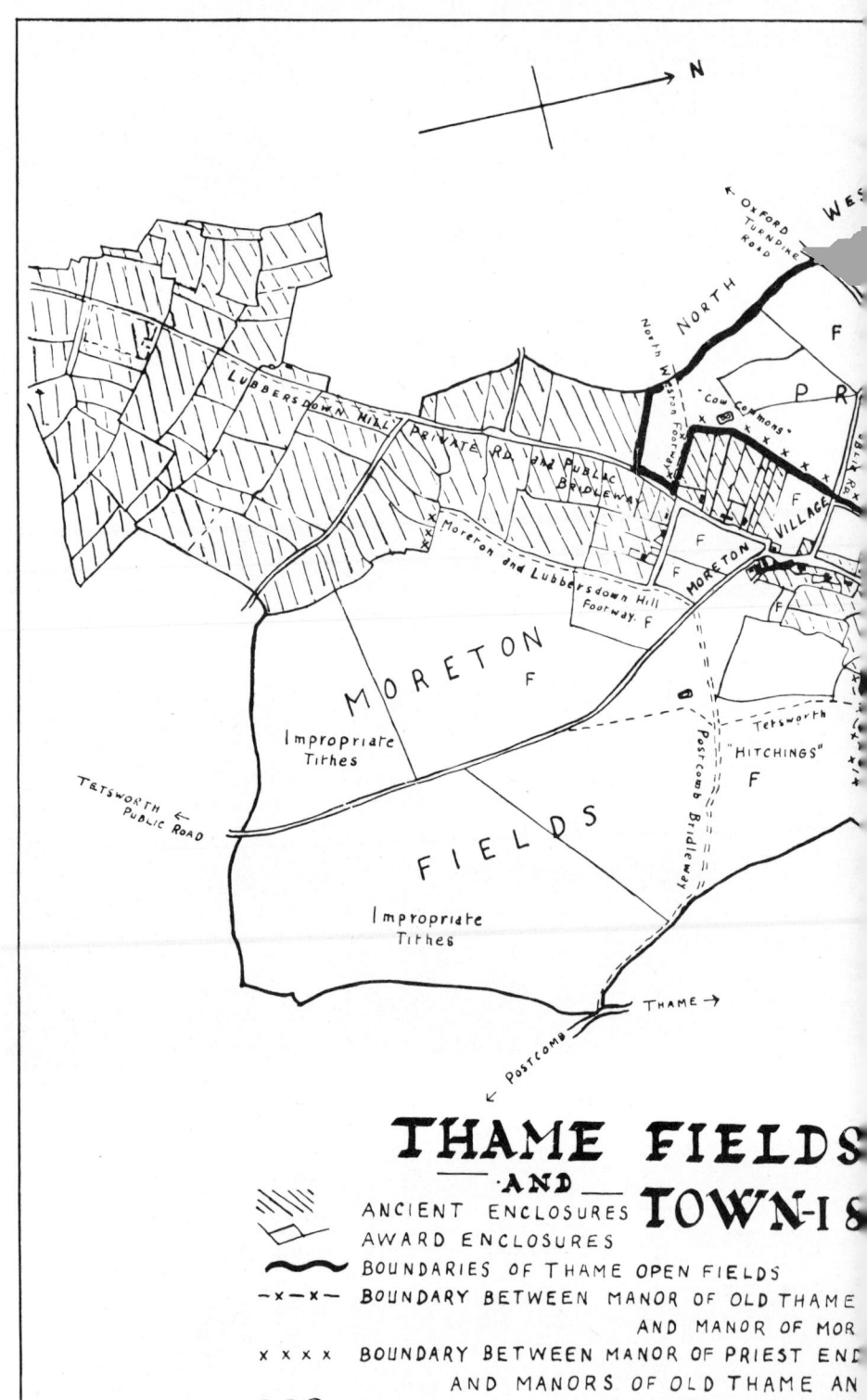

THAME FIELDS
·AND·
TOWN·18

ANCIENT ENCLOSURES
AWARD ENCLOSURES
BOUNDARIES OF THAME OPEN FIELDS
-x—x— BOUNDARY BETWEEN MANOR OF OLD THAME
AND MANOR OF MOR
x x x x BOUNDARY BETWEEN MANOR OF PRIEST END
AND MANORS OF OLD THAME AN
⊗ ⊗ ⊗ LIMIT OF THAME TOWN IN PRIEST END

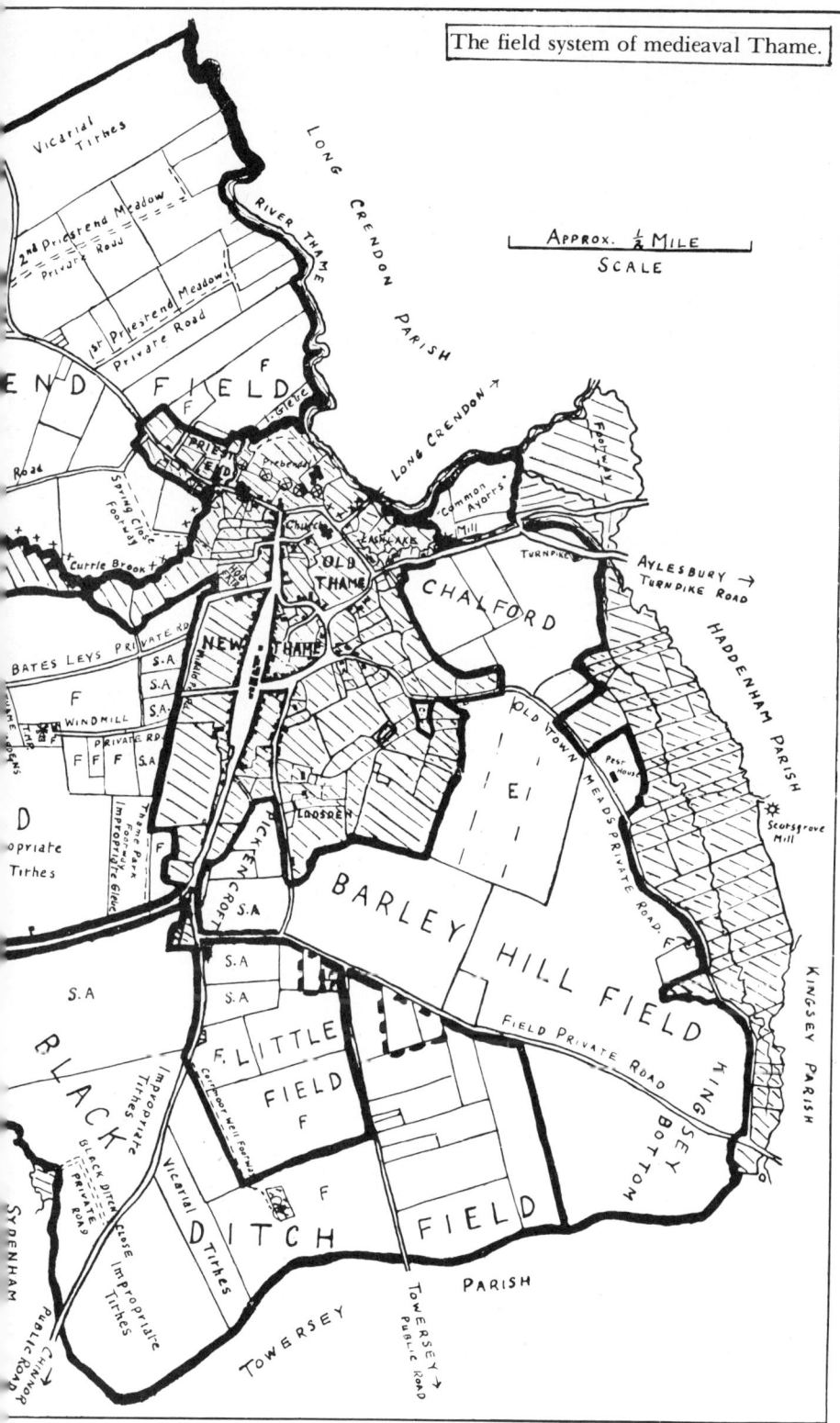

The field system of medieval Thame.

Approx. ⅛ Mile
SCALE

ABOVE: North Weston Manor House, home of the Quatremains, demolished in the last century. CENTRE: A picture of the earliest Market Hall: probably built in the 16th Century. BELOW: The second Market Hall, in 1880. The mysterious tower to the left appears to be part of the building, perhaps a staircase.

Abbey, Church and Prebendal

The earliest surviving parts of the present Parish Church probably date from the 1240s, when Bishop Grosseteste began an extensive rebuilding programme, but there were certainly earlier structures on the site. By 1146, Thame had become a Prebend of Lincoln Cathedral, and in the next century, a vicarage was endowed. The shape of these early churches is unknown, but the cruciform 13th century building still survives, admittedly much embellished.

St. Mary's Church has importance, not least because it represents the most substantial mediaeval building in Thame. In the 14th century, aisles and a South Porch were added, and in the 15th century, various alterations were effected, including the reconstruction of the North Transept from 1442. Much fascinating detail on this and other matters is contained in the Churchwardens' Accounts, which date from 1442. The total cost of the rebuilding was £28 15s 3d, including 3s for the plumber to 'turne ye spowte of ye stepul', 6d for makying of ye cloche', and 1d for a 'lokke to ye fante [font]'. The masons employed were provided with victuals at the Church's expense, and a subscription list of donors appears in the account!

A fair picture of the life and liturgy of a mediaeval parish church can be pieced together from this source. The church seems to have been well equipped with furnishings—surplices, altar cloths, veils, lanterns, cushions, communion vessels, and even a 'knife' to cut 'holy brede'. An inventory of 1447 also lists 21 books owned, including a legendum, or book of the lives of Saints and Martyrs. Organs and bells are frequently mentioned; a 'paynter of Buckyngham' received 20s for a picture of Mary in 1469, and a glazier was employed in 1477. To colour and sound was added an element of drama at festivals; rushes were provided at Pentecost, straw at Christmas, and a Whitsuntide play included a collection gathered by 'Robyn Hood'—legitimately, one hopes!

Bread and ale was provided for the choir and bell ringers on several occasions, to serenade visiting nobility or monarchs, such as Henry VIII in 1530. Not only did the Church serve as social centre for the parish, it also acted as social welfare agency. 12d was paid for paving the Market Place in 1550; Elizabeth Waye received money in 1551 'when her house was visited with the Plague', and two years earlier 16d was expended on a shroud for a poor man who had just died.

Meanwhile, the Church had been embellished with an ostentatious display of wealth and posthumous importance. Not only did the local nobility, like the

Quatremains family, erect large tombs to commemorate themselves, they also endowed chantry chapels and hired priests to say masses for their souls after death. The St Christopher Chantry (as the Quatremains donation was called), was in the North Transept; a priest was retained to hold regular masses. This arrangement ended in 1549, when the chantries were swept away. Symbolically, the largest monument in Thame Church belongs to Lord Williams, to whom the Chantry revenues were assigned.

Thame had been endowed by Bishop Grosseteste with a Prebend, an administrative sub-division of the Bishopric of Lincoln. The duties of the prebend included appointing to the living of Thame, and enforcement of canon law in the prebendal court. The office was obviously worth having, as a rather undignified squabble occurred in 1241, when Pope and Bishop both appointed to the office. In the same year, the Prebendal Chapel was constructed; the present living and domestic quarters were added later, including extensive lodging accommodation for visiting dignitaries. Some prebendaries were probably non-resident, holding the office in plurality with other lucrative positions, but others were benefactors of the Church. Richard Maudelay, prebend in 1529, for example, donated the present seats in the chancel. At the Reformation, the prebend was sold into private hands, along with the advowson.

However, one anomaly continued: the Parish remained a 'peculiar' of the Bishopric of Lincoln, even after the creation of the diocese of Oxford in 1542. The situation seems to have been equally confusing to contemporaries, several acrimonious exchanges occurring between the two dioceses over the centuries.

Church and prebendal served the town of Thame. Thame Abbey by contrast was autonomous. Indeed, the Cistercian monks who inhabited the monastery were renowned for their emphasis on self-sufficiency and isolation. The Abbey was founded in about 1140, after a false start on Otmoor. Only a few traces of the buildings remain—one small chapel, and the Abbot's lodging, incorporated in the present Mansion.

Originally, austerity and rigid discipline probably prevailed at the Abbey, but by the 15th century, the monastery seems to have fallen into a state of laxity. The Abbey grew rich, with an income of £141 in 1526. As the Abbey paid no tithes on land it worked itself, there was a great temptation to indulge in extensive commercial activities beyond the immediate needs of the community. In the case of Thame Abbey, sheep-farming was a major activity, and large areas were enclosed.

The symptoms of the weakness of the Catholic Church on the eve of the Reformation were thus visible in Thame, and the start of the rot was not too deep below the surface, as Lollardy was also prevelant in the Chilterns at the time. Thame's example was not unique: just across the Buckinghamshire border (but arguably part of Thame's story) was Notley Abbey, a house of Augustinian Canons which was visited by Bishop Alnwick in 1447. The Bishop found a sad state of affairs, with feuds between the Canons, drunkenness, slackness in the running of the

House, the Abbey Church in disrepair—even the novices sang painfully out of time due to lack of teaching! The aged Abbot Redying had obviously allowed things to slip. At the Dissolution in 1535, there were 14 occupants who were well pensioned.

But the weaknesses and failings in the Church as a whole were soon to be exposed and used for political gain. The Reformation was coming to Thame.

Thame Park; the Garden Front. The Abbot's lodging quarters were here.
From a print of 1868. (BL)

ABOVE: An aerial view of Thame Park, showing the monastic quarters.
BELOW LEFT: The Mediaeval Chapel at the Abbey as it was in 1868. (BL)
CENTRE: The Thame Hoard. (WM) RIGHT: The seal of a 13th century
Abbot.

ABOVE LEFT: A closer view of the ring in the Thame Hoard. RIGHT: Thame Church, showing the South Transept. BELOW: The Tithe Barn in Church Lane. Payment of tithes was much resented: the size of the barn suggests a bountiful income. (QPS)

ABOVE LEFT: Internal view of Thame Church 40 years ago, facing East. RIGHT: Thame Prebendal before restoration. Etching by H. Hinton, 1868. (BL).BELOW LEFT: A page from the Churchwarden's Accounts in the early 16th century (BL). RIGHT: A boathouse and punt in the Prebendal grounds.

ABOVE: An old bridge in the grounds of the Prebendal, long since disappeared. BELOW: The Chapel of the Prebendal in about 1920.

Lord Williams

The 16th century saw not only a religious revolution; momentous social changes occurred as well. To win loyalty, Henry VIII was desperately generous in his gifts of land and booty from the despoiled monasteries. The grateful recipients found their wealth and social prestige greatly enhanced. Many Tudor success stories began in the aftermath of the Monastic Dissolutions. John Williams, of Rycote, was one such case.

His father, also called John Williams, had perhaps gained certain political eminence by his marriage to a second cousin of Thomas Cromwell, and more tangible property in his second marriage to Elizabeth More, of Burghfield, Berkshire. John Williams was the younger son, born about 1500-3. His early life is obscure; he married about 1530 into a wealthy furrier's family, and had four children. Both his sons seemed to have pre-deceased him, in 1537, probably by the sweating sickness. His two daughters achieved greater longevity. Margery, the younger, became a favourite of Queen Elizabeth, earning the endearing nickname 'my own crow'.

John Williams achieved political eminence, initially in Wolsey's administration as Principal Clerk to the King's Jewels (1531) and later as Master of the Jewels, surviving the fall of his protégé Thomas Cromwell in 1540. He was granted a knighthood in 1537, as befitted the holder of a venerable office of state, and seems to have found royal favour attending functions at Court, such as the christening of Henry's long awaited son Edward in 1537, and the greeting of Anne of Cleves at Dover later that year. Another curious side of his office involved the supply of 'cramp rings' blessed by the King, as protection against the affliction. Henry VIII apparently monopolised so much of the realm's gold and silver that the supply of these rings was infrequent, and consequently Williams was able to exert valuable patronage. Late in Henry's reign, he was made Chief Supervisor of all Swans—a singular honour.

National prestige was matched by local honours for Sir John Williams. He had purchased Rycote House in 1539, and served in turn as Justice of the Peace, Sheriff of the County, and Member of Parliament. After showing tenacity in the King's service when enquiring into the seditious aspects of the Pilgrimage of Grace, he was appointed as visitor to the Monasteries in 1539. In this capacity he accepted the surrender of Thame Abbey that year.

He was related by marriage to the last Abbott, Robert King, and his personal feelings about the Dissolution are difficult to assess. On the one hand, he wrote slightingly about 'all the roten bones that be called reliques' and commented enviously on the accumulated monastic gold and silver. Yet in 1552, he was imprisoned in the Fleet for a short time for giving pensions to dispossessed monks without the sanction of the Privy Council. He may simply have viewed the job as a necessary administrative task; the royal grant of land at Thame Abbey in 1542 must certainly have eased any qualms. Moreover, as Treasurer of the Court of Augmentations from 1544, he had responsibility for the administration of revenues for the King from the dissolved monasteries. There is every reason to believe that he found the post profitable! His relation, Abbot King, fared equally well, becoming Bishop of Oxford, and (like Williams) survived the reigns of both Edward VI and Mary.

At the dissolution of Thame Abbey in 1539, 10 monks plus the Abbot, Prior and Sub-Prior signed the surrender to Sir John. The inhabitants of Thame were probably enviously hostile towards the Abbey, whose wealth was assessed at £256 13s 7d, and whose Abbots had within living memory rebuilt their own Lodging Quarters in sumptuous style. Complaints had been made in 1525 that the Abbey was 'full of idle boys', and the Bishop of Lincoln in the same year fulminated against the Abbot as 'ignorant and useless'. Though Abbot King (who was appointed in 1529), may have improved standards, the Abbey had done little to endear itself locally, and its substantial enclosing of land, and its privileges, may have earned it many enemies.

Edward VI's reign brought further far-reaching religious changes to Thame. In 1547, the Prebendary was surrendered into private hands, and the endowment of Chantries of St. Christopher in the parish church and at Rycote Chapel were given to Sir John Williams. A spate of legislation established the Protestant Anglican Church. The Churchwardens had already seen the writing on the wall, for in 1549 they had personally taken charge of the Parish Church's portable valuables. The Churchwardens' accounts tell the sorry tale of the dispersal of these precious articles to the value of £300, including the 'Great Bell' sold for £23 13s 11d, and the High Altar Cross for £22 4s. Altars and Rood Screens were dismantled. On 3 May 1557, 8d was expended 'for sendying for the Crowner (Coroner) to sitt upon laborer that felle out of the Rode loft & dyed'—a suitable end for an iconoclast? Books of Homilies, Psalms and Erasmus' *Paraphrases* were purchased for the new religion.

However, this radical phrase was brought to an abrupt end in 1553 on the death of the boy-King Edward. Sir John Williams, shortly to become Lord Williams, proclaimed Mary as Queen in the county. He had steadily slid out of favour with Edward's advisers, culminating in his imprisonment, so it was doubtless with loyal relief that he welcomed the new Queen. However, as a Catholic, Mary could hardly be expected to tolerate Protestant dogma and institutions, and Sir John's position as Treasurer of the Court of Augmentations disappeared. However, new honours replaced this loss. He was appointed Lord Chamberlain upon Mary's marriage to Philip of Spain. Moreover, he was given charge of Princess Elizabeth, but his exceptional leniency and courtesy led to her transfer to stricter Guardians. But Mary was treading dangerously; her Spanish marriage proved desperately unpopular, and her attempt to compel a return to Catholicism by force and and persecution exacerbated this unpopularity. At Oxford, three recalcitrant Bishops were tried in 1555, and Williams, as Sheriff, received the royal command to be present at the two burnings, as depicted by Foxe. Bloody Mary's death in 1558 opened the way for more moderate government, and further honours for Sir John.

Elizabeth appointed her kind captor as President of the Council of the Welsh Marches, an important administrative and judicial position. His tenure of office was however brief: weighed down perhaps by the recent deaths of his sons and wife and his prison confinement, he died at Ludlow Castle on 14 October 1559. His Will amply demonstrates the extent of his wealth and power—30 Manors, 156 lb of plate, 22 horses and extensive numbers of livestock. His funeral at Thame on 15 November was a splendidly solemn occasion, and his large marble tomb in Thame Church—centrally placed in the Chancel—serves as a permanent reminder of his importance, along with the School founded by his Will which bears his name. His possessions at Thame were dispersed into various branches of the family. Thame Park, the former Abbey, was occupied by his elder daughter Isobel and her husband, Sir Richard Wenman. Rycote passed to his younger daughter, Margery who married Sir Henry Norreys. The House became a favourite resting place of Queen Elizabeth, and Margery a particular favourite (and lady-in-waiting) of the Queen.

Lord Williams was undoubtedly a minor figure in Elizabethan political history. He served conscientiously under four contrasting regimes, one of a core of loyal administrators to the English Crown. He succeeded in subordinating personal prejudices to the greater task of serving the monarch and the law. He could thus reconcile his part in the plunder of the monasteries with his role in the burnings of the Bishops. There were many others who found it necessary to perform gymnastics of conscience to survive in this troubled period of the Tudors. However, the minor administrator was also a major figure locally in Thame, and in the County of Oxford for, as a landowner, Member of Parliament and Sheriff he represented both nationally. The posthumous fame of his name belongs to another chapter.

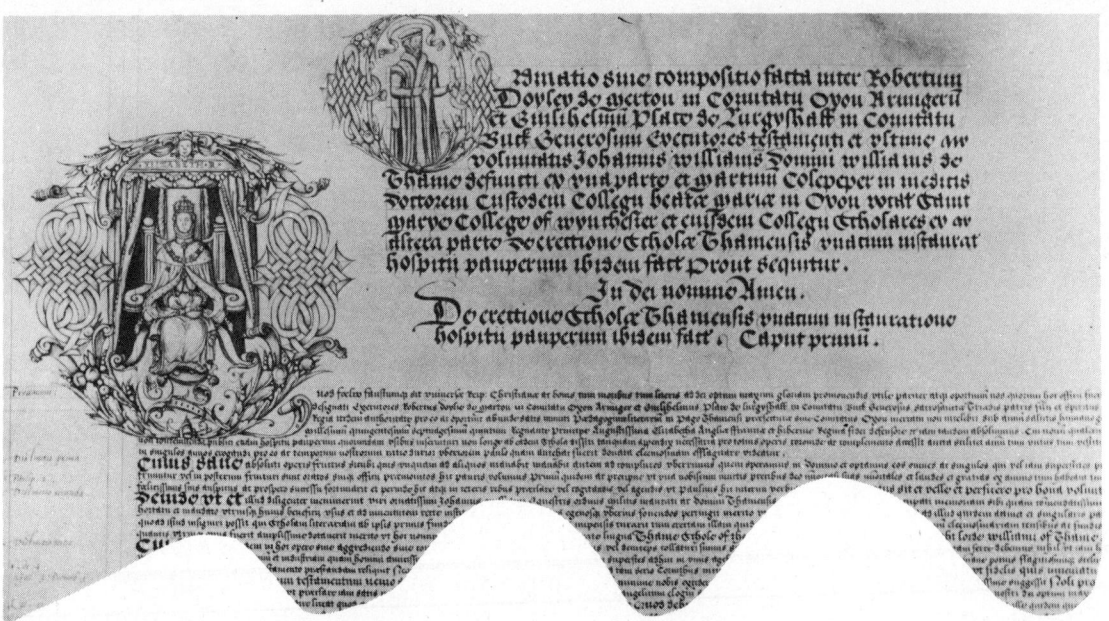

ABOVE: A copy of the school statutes of 1575. A picture of Lord Williams appears in the elaborate top figure, and of Queen Elizabeth in the other. BELOW: Signature of Lord Williams.

Lord Williams's crest: the origin of the crossed organ pipes is obscure. (QPS)

A Table defcribing the burning of B. Ridley, and Father Latimer at Oxford, I
there preaching at the time of their Martyrdome.

Si corpus meum tradi ig-
ni, caritaté auté non ha-
beam, nihil util tatis, &c

O Lord ftrengthen them.

Smith

Father of Heaven re-
ceive my foul.

Latimer   Ridley

In manus tuas domine.

Maſter Ridley, I will re-
member your ſuit.

L. Withā.

Place this between *Fol.* 502. and 503. Voll. 3.

ABOVE: The Burning of the Oxford Martyrs in 1556. Lord Williams, as
sheriff, was responsible for its organisation. CENTRE and BELOW:
Tudor clothes, found during alterations to a shop. Two sets of shoes, some
gloves, a clay pipe and a hat. RIGHT: Letter from Lord Williams to
Thomas Cromwell in June 1539.

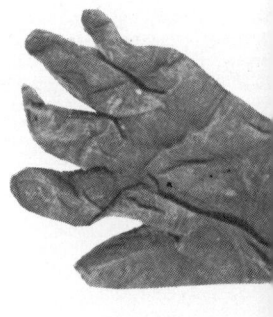

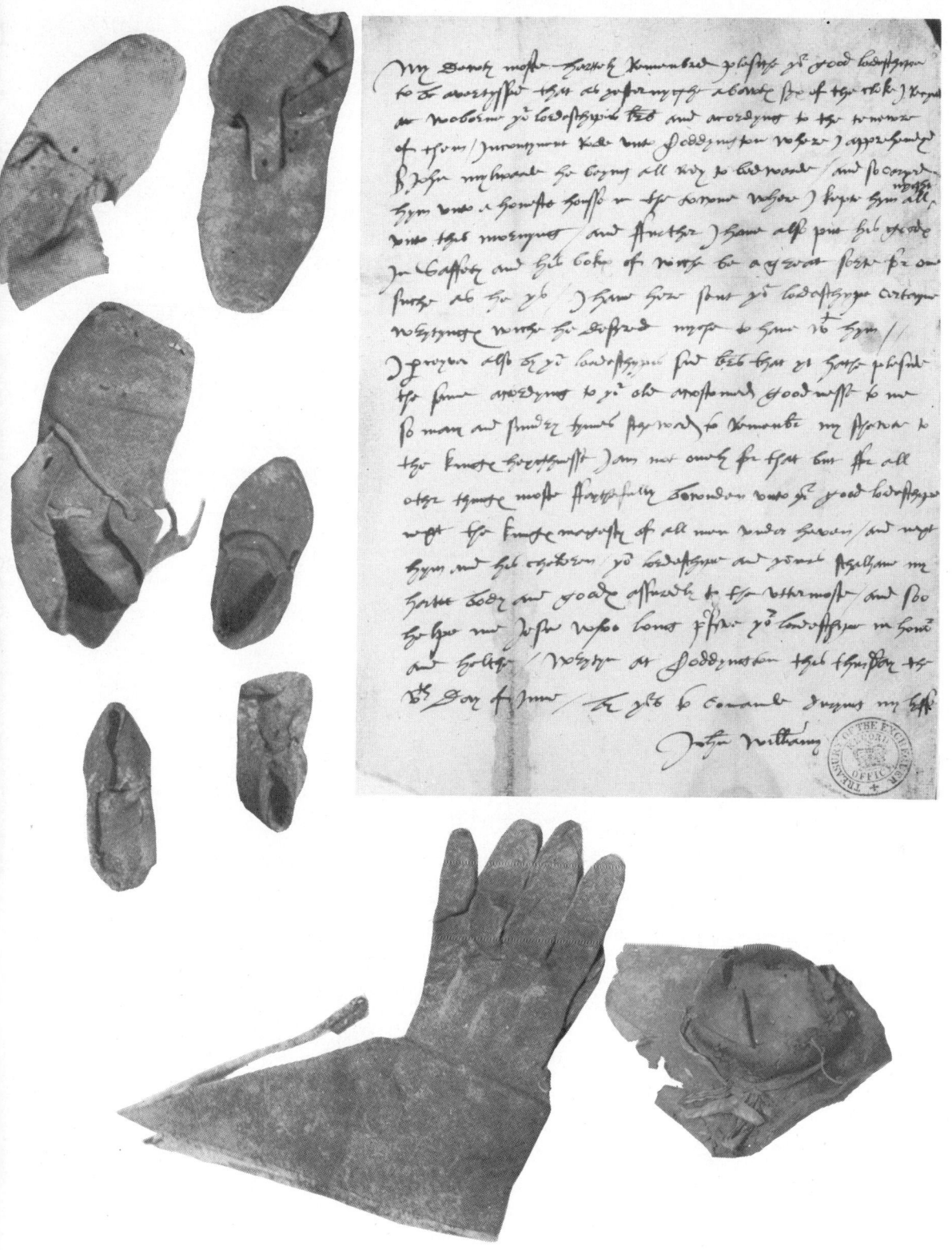

ABOVE: Tudor wall-painting from a house in High Street, Thame, discovered in an attic. (OMS). BELOW: The house in which the painting was found (QPS).

Lord Williams's Legacy

By his Will of 18 March 1559, Lord Williams bequeathed property to sustain 'a free School in the Town of Thame'. The yield was £47 4s 4d a year, most of which was gobbled up by salaries for the Master and his Assistant. A further £9 18s 1d went towards the re-endowment of the Almhouses. Lord Williams could well afford these sums which were but drops in the ocean compared with his personal family bequests. But the fact the he chose charitable endowment is significant—whether it was out of conviction or conscience is for speculation.

The School building in Church Lane was apparently erected in 1569, and teaching began soon after, though the Statutes, which regulated the School's operation, were not issued until 1575, when the endowment was handed over to the Warden and Fellows of New College, Oxford, to ensure the proper and continuing function of the School. The School and College were therefore recently able to celebrate 400 years of association.

The T-shaped building provided accommodation for the two teachers and about 40 to 50 pupils. Private rooms existed for the staff, but the boarders had to sleep in the draughty attics. A large School room was the only other area provided.

The conduct of the School was strictly controlled by the Statutes. The master was paid £26 13s 4d a year in salary and his duties compared to those of the captain in 'this ship of learning'. He, or his appointed assistant, known as the Usher, always had to be present at the School apart from one month's holiday. The first Headmaster Edward Harris was in charge from 1570 to 1600; his brass in the Church shows him in his academic robes. Like many subsequent masters he was educated at New College, and the post tended to become a sinecure for Fellows of New College.

The 16th Century schoolboy had a hard life by modern standards. Pupils at Lord Williams's were expected to attend School from 6.00 am to 11.00 am and 1.00 pm to 6.00 pm (an hour earlier in Winter). The boys had to pay for candles to light their gloom during those dim hours, and also for cleaning materials, and 'rods' for them to be punished with. By all accounts knowledge was frequently beaten in rather than imparted, although the Statutes contained a specific instruction that chastisement was to be confined to the nether quarters and not the head.

Study was intensive; boys entered the School at about the age of 7 and left after six years of drilling in Latin (even the instruction was given in Latin—the direct method.) Prefects were appointed to assist the teachers. In addition, religious observance was strictly circumscribed; daily prayers were said 'for inculcating piety or for checking the frivolity of the young' and on Sundays and festivals the whole School would troop up to the Church and assemble round the Founder's tomb. A test was given on the sermon upon return to ensure proper attention was paid. By the turn of the Century, the Grammar School was well established; in 1610 William Camden the antiquarian described it as 'a very faire schole'.

The other part of Lord Williams's benefaction, the Almhouses were also thriving by this time. The five old men and one old woman had to wear gowns 'of Lyon tawney cloth of Reading make' lined with black lambskin, on festival occasions. They too had to pay Sunday homage round their founder's tomb, but there was an extra incentive, for they received 6d a week for attending. The old woman was expected to nurse the others in infirmity, and as a special privilege the 'most ancient almsman' was paid 4s to clean the drains running from the 'privy' in the orchard of the School.

Meanwhile, Lord Williams's heirs continued the traditions of hospitality at his seats of Thame Park and Rycote. Queen Elizabeth followed up her 'captive' visit of 1554 on four other occasions—and threatened more. On one occasion in 1572, the Earl of Leicester was unfortunate enough to be the bearer of the annoying tidings that, after weeks of preparation, the Queen had decided not to come. He was consigned to the stables that wet and windy night for his pains! Elizabeth seems to have held the House and its occupants in special favour, however, and wrote a touching note to Lady Norreys in 1597 upon the death of her husband in Ireland: 'Let these lines from your gracious and loving Sovereign serve to assure you that there shall ever appear the lively characters of you and yours that are left, in valuing all their faithful and honest endeavours'–Lord Williams's legacy was truly great.

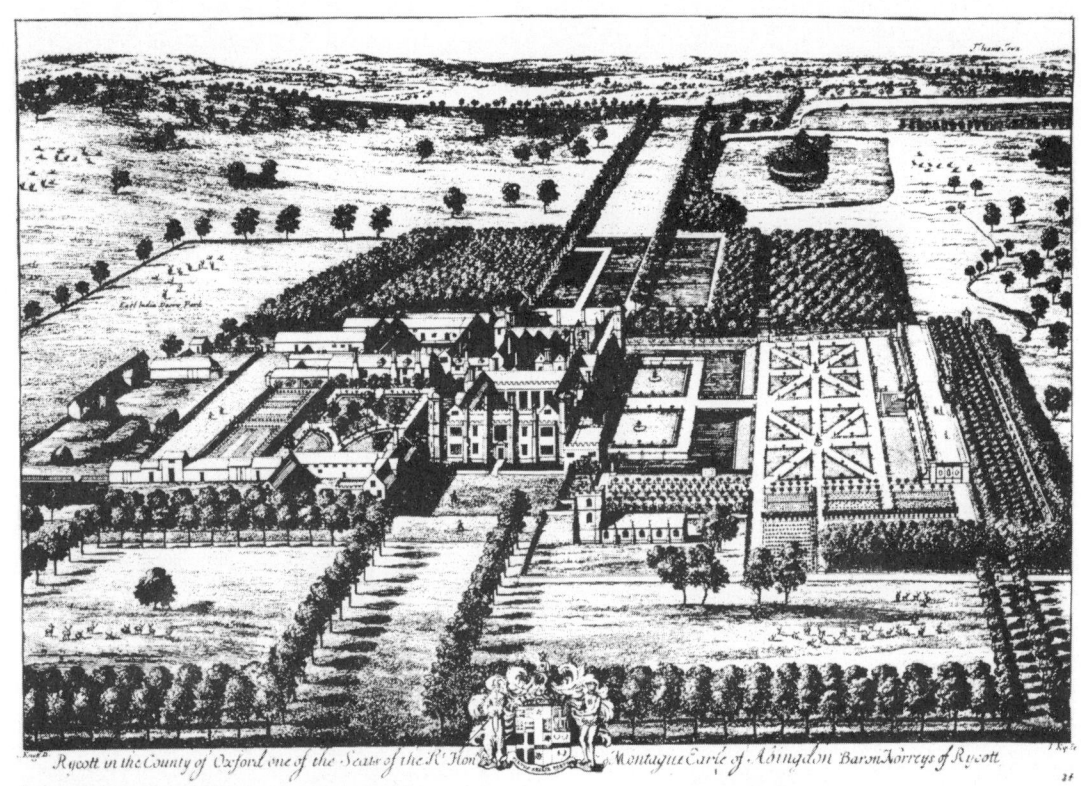

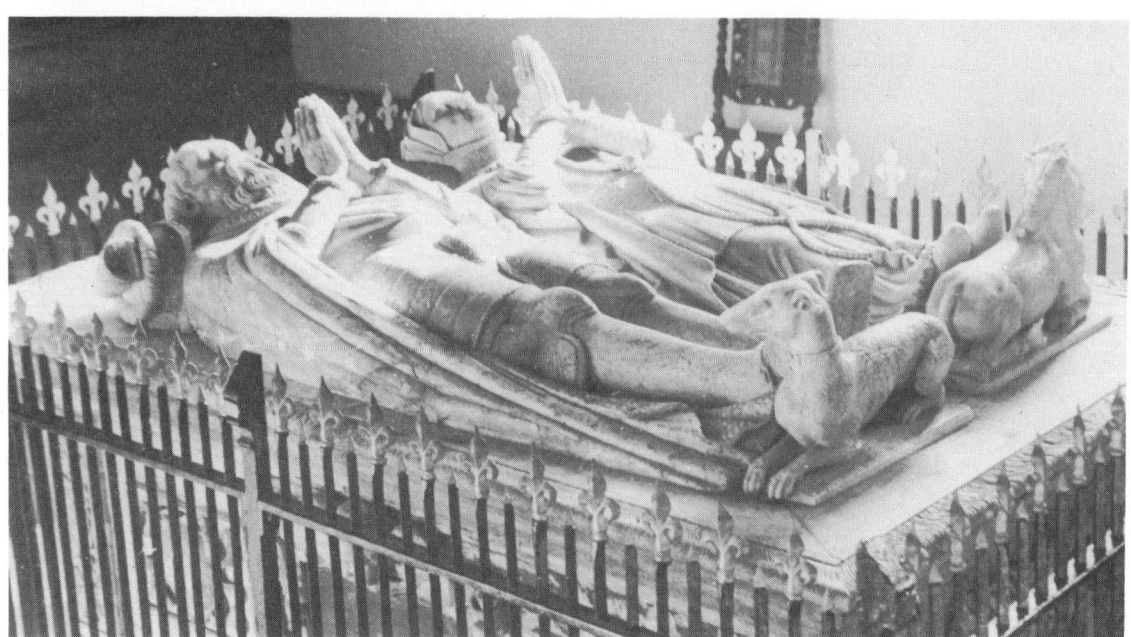

ABOVE: Rycote House, home of Lord Williams. From a view by Kip.
BELOW: Lord Williams' tomb in Thame Parish Church. (QPS)

ABOVE: The main front of Rycote House during the 18th Century.
BELOW: The remains of Rycote House in 1868.

ABOVE: Lord Williams' School, as founded by his will in 1559. BELOW LEFT: Edward Harris, first headmaster of the School. Taken from his brass in Thame Church. RIGHT: Richard Boucher, Headmaster 1597-1627. Hampden's teacher, under whose rule the school benches were 'crowded with youths eager to be taught'.

ABOVE: Portrait of John Hampden. BELOW: Hampden's spur. (AshM)

Divided Loyalties

The stability of Elizabeth's reign gradually crumbled under the Early Stuart monarchs as Crown and Parliament lurched towards war. However, there seem to have been few visible signs in early 17th century Thame of the growing tensions. Continuity with the past was strong; Royalty continued to visit Rycote House, and the beautiful Chapel was at this time enriched by the addition of family pews, one complete with a canopied ceiling of stars. *Sic itur ad astra?* The Churchwardens' Accounts continue to illuminate the affairs of the Church; a new Communion Table was purchased in 1625 (it still stands); the pulpit was mended with a seat, lockable door and hour-glass; a man was paid 2d in 1629 to keep dogs out of the Church. Meanwhile, the Grammar School flourished, and the Market thrived.

But beneath the surface, tensions were building up. The Norreys family at Rycote had near been extinguished in the service of Elizabeth's armies. Francis Norreys, the owner, had in 1621 been committed to the Fleet Prison in London on a charge of manslaughter. Though released in 1622, he committed suicide with a crossbow at Rycote. His daughter married well enough to be able to play host to Charles I at the manor, but by then the monarchy itself was under attack.

Long-term grievances were stoked into major issues to cause the outbreak of the English Civil War. The long-term conflict of authority between Crown and Parliament crystallised around such an issue as Ship Money. Charles' bluff was most strongly called in this area, and opposition to the tax, led by John Hampden (who was educated at Lord Williams's) became so powerful that it was virtually impossible to collect it in the County. The Sheriff of Oxfordshire complained that 'the County (was) generally adverse to pay' and though the King won a technical victory in the Law Courts, the loss of authority was fatal as the country drifted towards Civil War.

Thame found itself with divided loyalties in the conflict. Oxford was the regional centre for the king, whilst Aylesbury was firmly in parliamentary hands. Thus, both Roundheads and Cavaliers found themselves in Thame. Anthony Wood, the diarist, at school in Thame during the Civil War, thought the town's sentiments leaned towards the Parliamentary side. Certainly, the vicar, the Rev. Tennant, was a man of Puritan sympathies. In the early stages of the war, Prince Rupert wavered in the assaults on Aylesbury, falling back on Thame. The Parliamentary troops attempted to use Thame as a base for an assault on Oxford, but were thwarted by

Rupert's sniping raids.

On 17 June 1643, Rupert was lured from Oxford by reports of a Parliamentary pay chest in the area. Failing to trace it, he assailed and plundered Chinnor instead. On the return to Oxford, he met some hastily assembled Parliamentary forces at Chalgrove. John Hampden was one of this force, and during the skirmish he was mortally wounded. Whether his fatal wounds were sustained in action, or the result of his own gun exploding upon him is debatable, according to whose side of the story one accepts. However, it is more or less certain that he repaired to the comforts of the Greyhound Inn at Thame to nurse his wounds. He expired there on 24 June, and was buried at Great Hampden Church. An obelisk was erected at Chalgrove in 1843 to commemorate the battle and its most famous victim, whilst Aylesbury honoured him with a statue in the Market Place. Thame, whilst glad to accept his reputation, has only a tablet, erected in this century by members of the old Girls' Grammar School.

Strangely enough, with all this action going on, in 1644 two young brothers from Oxford arrived in Thame, to be educated at Lord Williams's School. The diaries of the 12 year old Anthony Wood provide interesting information on the Civil War period. War seemed always near at hand. In January 1644, he witnessed 'a great number of horsemen pushing towards Thame over Crendon Bridge, and in the head of them was Blagge [Royalist Colonel of Wallingford Castle] with a bloody face' and Roundheads in hot pursuit. In September 1644, the two sides met in open skirmish on the streets of Thame, again witnessed by Wood. Legend has it that a motley collection of human and animal skeletons found in a local field in 1885 represent the residual remains of this carnage.

Action in the streets occurred again in April 1645, when the royalist Commander of Boarstall House despatched a troop of horse and gained the edge of an encounter at 'the bridge below Thame Mill'. In September 1645, the Parliamentary troops barricaded the town with carts. However, the arrival of 400 of Prince Rupert's cavalry caught them with their pants down (literally), and the Royalists were able to engage in some gentle pillage. However, no great casualties seem to have been sustained in any of these encounters, and Anthony Wood and his schoolmates were actually given the day off to watch the surrender of Boarstall garrison in June 1646.

Thame was thus again a frontier, reflecting changing fortunes, but by 1646, Charles' war was over. Thame had time to count the cost. The Church seems to have suffered most. Troops, horses and prisoners were quartered there, and some damage was done to Lord Williams's tomb ('very much mangled and broken') which was repaired in 1661. Lord Essex's troops were also alleged to have laid into the organ and 'went tooting about the town with the pipes'. Extensive billeting seems to have occurred, especially in the School House.

But this latter institution had a remarkable resilience, for the Civil War period produced the greatest ever concentration of famous pupils at the school. Mention has already been made of John Hampden and Anthony Wood. In addition, John

Holt, later Lord Chief Justice of England received some of his education there. Brown and Guest describe him as 'the greatest man the town has ever produced', and he certainly had a great reputation in his lifetime for fairness and honesty, and was not afraid to take on the might of both Houses of Parliament.

Other famous (or notorious) old boys of the school at this time include William Lenthall, Speaker of the Long Parliament; Bishop Henry King of Chichester; assorted academics, including Edward Pocock, an early scholar of the Orient, and Dr. John Fell, Dean of Christ Church, memorable largely through the famous epigram about him:

'I do not like you, Dr. Fell,
But why, I cannot tell.
But this I know full well
I do not love you, Dr. Fell.'

Two regicides, Sir Richard Ingolsby and Simon Mayne, were also educated at Lord Williams (confirming perhaps the Puritan bias of the schoolmaster), as was Shakerley Marmion, the dramatist. There is insufficient evidence that Sir George Etherege (author of the play *Love in a Tub)* was an old boy; he has probably been confused with a local family of that name who are known to have attended the school.

How much they all owed to the school is debatable; Anthony Wood recorded that 'I have come under the discipline of the rod twice in a forenoon, which yet brake no bones'. One is reminded of the ancient Egyptian saying that 'the ear of the boy is on his backside, and he hearkeneth when he is beaten'. Yet even the sore-bottomed Wood admitted that the school 'was in good reputation'. However, repairs were necessary after the war, and the schooling in those years appears to have been intermittent. The Golden Age was coming to an end.

William Lenthall

House
of Ezekiel
Browne
at Thame
in which John
Hampden
died —

See p. 133 of
these Collections
for an account
of the sale of
this house

ABOVE : The Greyhound Inn, where John Hampden died in 1643, as drawn by Lee in 1846. (BM) BELOW Anthony Wood, diarist.

ABOVE: Close up of Lord Williams' marble tomb. It was repaired after damage in the Civil War.
BELOW: John Fell, Bishop of Oxford.

Some famous old boys of the school. LEFT: Sir John Holt, Lord Chief Justice. ABOVE RIGHT: George Croke, Justice of the King's Bench, who ended his career by deciding against the king in a ship money case. BELOW: Edward Pocock, 'a scholar whose learning was the admiration of Europe'.

54

The Land

The process by which the mediaeval feudal system became eroded was gradual. The date of the final enclosure of the open fields in Thame, 1823, is rather late as these things go, especially when one considers that the first enclosing had taken place some 700 years earlier in 1140 when permission was granted to the monks to enclose part of the area of Thame Park.

However, the open-field system of agriculture, with its emphasis on cultivation in long strips of land, became increasingly anachronistic as the years went on. The feudal bond, based on loyalty and duty, declined in importance from the era of the Plague, when labour became scarce and money wages began to replace serfdom. We have no specific knowledge of the effect of the Plague locally and no significant depopulation can be detected, but other facts were conspiring to undermine the feudal system. Enclosures for sheep were common in the area. The villages of Attington, Copcourt, North Weston and the two Rycotes disappeared in this way during the latter half of the Middle Ages, largely due to the energies of local magnates in search of wool profit: John Clerk of North Weston, for example, was granted (or rather purchased) a pardon in 1538 for the 'ruin, decay and violent destruction' of the hamlet. The Dormers and Quatremains also enclosed extensively, as did the Cistercian Monks at Thame Abbey.

Officially, the Government attitude towards enclosure was hostile, and there was a plethora of anti-enclosure laws passed during the 15th and 16th Centuries. However, there was little political mileage to be had from alienating the prosperous land owners and merchants at a time when the wool trade was booming, and often enclosing was overlooked and only derisory 'punishments' were imposed upon offenders.

However, in an area of extensive enclosure, Thame itself remained virtually intact until the early 19th Century. The situation was complex, for Thame had no less than five separate groups of fields by the 15th Century—Old Thame, New Thame, Moreton-with-Attington, North Weston and Priest End. By the 19th Century, Attington and North Weston had been enclosed, Priest End was reduced to one field, and the Thame fields organised into three large areas. Common grazing land existed along the banks of the Thame and Cuttlebrook Streams.

The 1823 enclosure award is a bulky document, covering Thame and Sydenham, a total of 2,180 acres. The major landowners, Sophia Wykeham (later Baroness

55

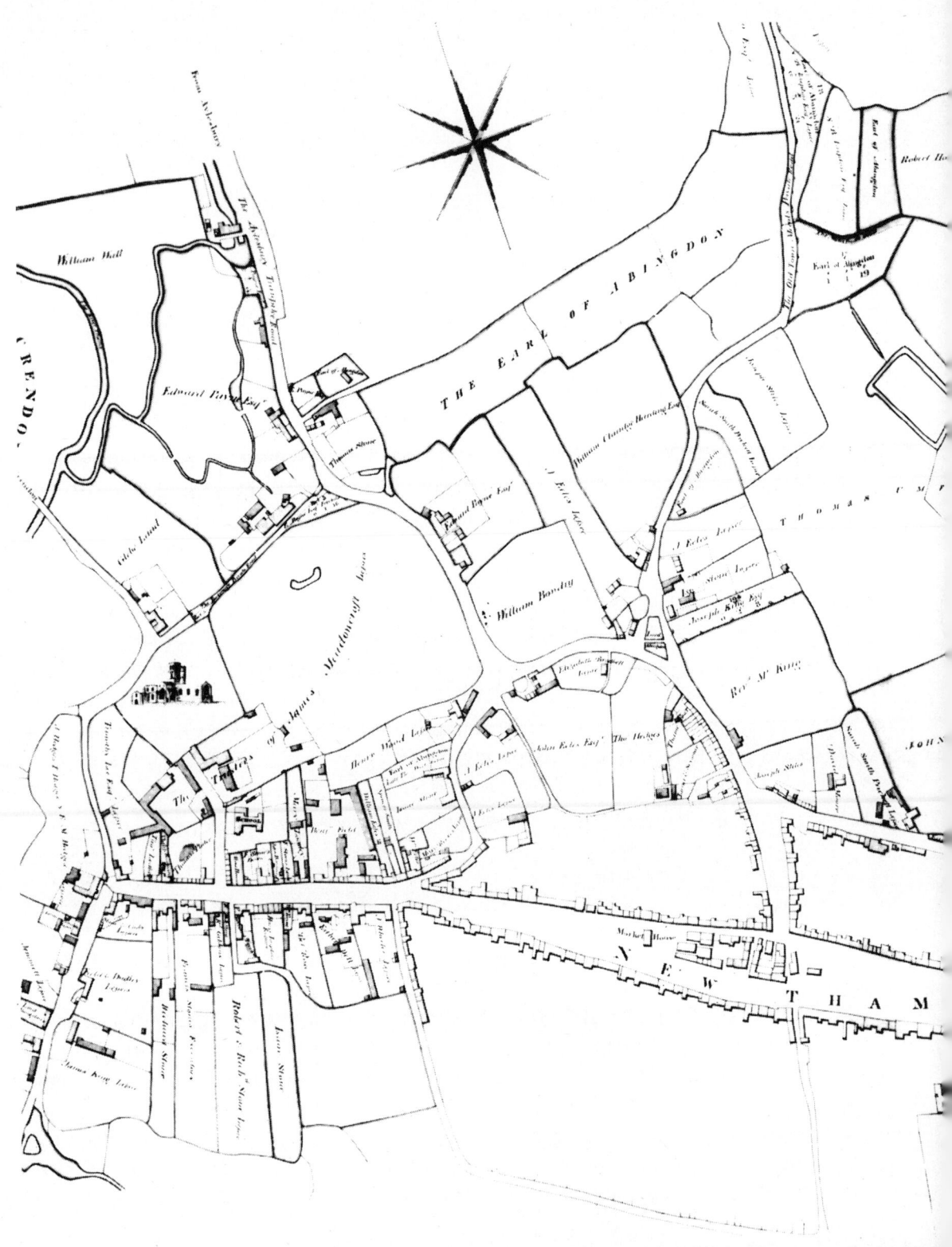

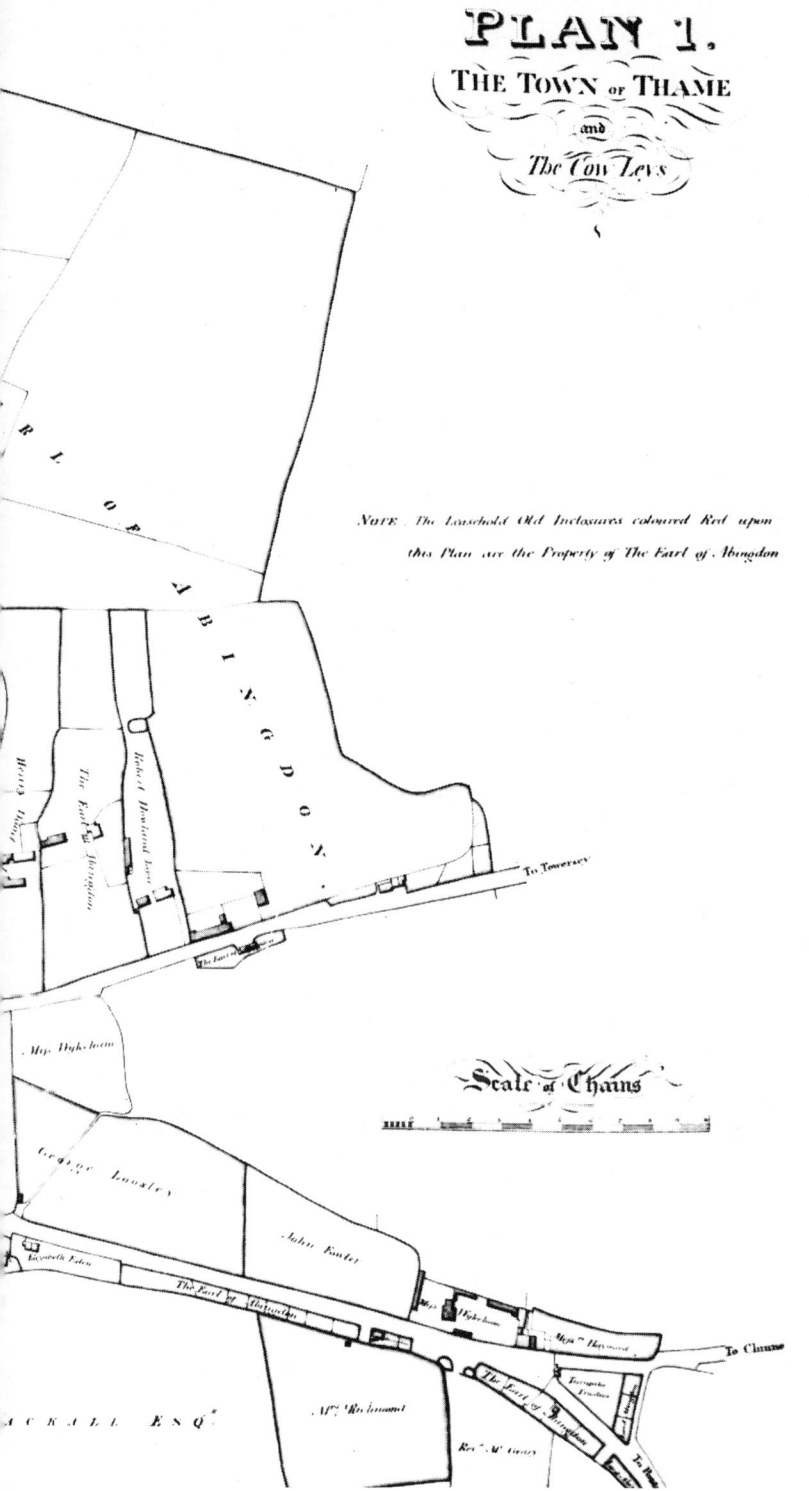

PLAN 1.

THE TOWN OF THAME

and

The Cow Leys

NOTE. The Leasehold Old Inclosures coloured Red upon this Plan are the Property of The Earl of Abingdon

The map from the Thame Enclosure Award, 1823. (OCRO)

Scale of Chains

Wenman) and the Earl of Abingdon, had petitioned for enclosure, and by this time the advantages of redrawing the land ownership map along more logical and economical lines were generally accepted. Lupton thought the enclosure brought great prosperity to the town, but then he did very well out of it, obtaining land adjacent to the Chinnor Road which was later developed for housing. The two major landowners fared well, as did Balliol and New College who had fairly extensive land holdings locally. The Vicar secured a generous glebe allotment of 180 acres in return for giving up his tithe rights. The Churchwardens acquired 6 acres in Bates Leys for charitable purposes, and some land near the windmill was put aside for use by the poor as allotments. As the land was of poor quality, this was a rather muted act of generosity.

There is, however, no especial reason to believe that the freeholders and allotment owners, who together held over half the land in question, gained much by the award. The freeholders, for example, had to cope with the expense of fencing their land, and some ended with a net reduction in area. The copyholders too, suffered from a diminution in their land, and some tenants still had land parcels scattered around in different fields.

What effect did the enclosure award have on a predominantly rural society like Thame? There can be little doubt that the Award tidied up the haphazard system of tenancy and ownership inherited from the Middle Ages. Large areas were more convenient to farm, and the 19th century was to bring many mechanical contrivances to these larger fields, replacing the horses and oxen. However, the changes ranged farther than this. The traditional crop rotation system in the area at the time of the 19th century was generally a four yearly one. The land lay fallow the first year, during the second year wheat was cultivated, in the third beans, pease, oats or tares and in the fourth barley or oats. Turnips and clover sometimes figured in this rotation, following in the wake of the agricultural innovators of the time. However, during the century, the area produced less corn, and Thame, once a 'great corn market' moved gradually to livestock. The change may well have been due to factors like the Corn Law Repeal of 1846 rather than to enclosure.

If methods and crops changed quite dramatically, so did the material circumstances of many of the workers on the land. The two decades preceding the award had witnessed an escalation of poverty on a gigantic scale. The poor rate in the county jumped from 1s 9d to 9s between 1786 and 1820. By 1811, £3,686 was needed each year for the poor. Arthur Young the traveller commented on Thame's 'very depressing poverty' and undoubtedly factors like this were influential in the national decision to change to a workhouse system in 1834. Enclosure probably exacerbated an already dismal situation, and under such circumstances, tempers became frayed. On nearby Otmoor, militant cottagers destroyed enclosure fences in 1829. A benevolent crowd rescued them from the militia at St. Giles' Fair, and fences continued to suffer moonlight depredations. Agricultural distress mingled freely with Ludditism and radical propaganda in the years 1829-1832, as England teetered on the brink of revolution. A winnowing machine was destroyed by a mob at Long Crendon in 1831. The violence abated after 1832, with the advent of the Reform Bill and Chartism, but rural poverty remained an inescapable fact of life for areas such as Thame, even during the prosperous years of the mid 19th century. Joseph Arch visited the area in 1876 and his Agricultural Labourer's Union had some local support.

This century, the decline in the agricultural working population has continued and the rural areas like Thame tended barely to sustain their population figures until the last 30 years. In 1914, 76% of of the land in the parish was pasture, and 23% arable. These figures were wholly unchanged in 1952, though there seems to have been a swing away from pig-farming locally.

The market continues to act as the focus for agriculture for the area. In the mid 19th century cattle, sheep and pigs and dairy products were its main goods. From 1865 (with the advent of the railway), milk for London came to have an increasing importance.

But the market was not ideally situated for the changing circumstances of the day. In 1865, 1877, 1883 and 1894 it was closed due to outbreaks of disease, and under dire threat of closure from the Board of Agriculture, the High Street area was properly paved in 1903 with a surface that could be washed and disinfected. Posts and chains for tethering were erected later, and can be seen on some old photographs. The tolls for pennage went to Sir Francis Bertie who had taken the re-paving initiative. In 1978, the Urban District Council took over the market rights and was collecting them. An interesting technicality connected with stallage charges frees the modern motorist from paying for car parking on the market, as ratepayers of the town are exempt from the fee. The Council leases the market to a firm of auctioneers, who pay a toll.

The shortcomings of the market had long been realised, and plans to move it to a more suitable site were finally brought to fruition in 1951, when the present site in North Street was taken over. The lease is due to expire soon, and the future of Thame's Cattle Market may hang in the balance. However, the Retail Market has benefited much from the extra space gained by its move from Cornmarket to Upper High Street, and continues to flourish.

Thame, as the natural focus for the area, can never shed its agricultural ties, but there is no doubt that the development of the town in recent years and the arrival (on a small scale as yet) of industry, will naturally weaken these historic links.

ABOVE Thame Park in the 18th Century. The house was totally refronted at this time. BELOW: The tomb of Lady Wenman. She feared burial alive, so her coffin was not interred and a device to filter air was incorporated in the lid.

Overhead views of Thame, showing the Church area and High Street.

61

ABOVE: A rural scene: threshing machines at South Weston. (OMS)
BELOW: Excavations at The Moats in Thame. The results were not
conclusive, but evidence of a 17th century water system was uncovered.
(OMS)

ABOVE: Thame Mill, by the riverside, while still in use. BELOW: The
windmill on the Moreton road.

Two views of Thame Cattle Market, before its removal to North Street,

ABOVE: Henry Taunt's famous photograph of Thame's Sheep Market.
BELOW: Thame Show. (QPS)

ABOVE: Thame Show. (QPS) BELOW: The amusement fair in High
Street. (QPS)

ABOVE: The weekly Tuesday market in Upper High Street. (QPS)
BELOW: A sheep auction in modern surroundings. (QPS)

1896
Ap.
May 4 The whole morning devoted to an examination of the work appointed to be done by St. II. by Ap. 30th. The Arithmetic was disastrous, not one quarter of the children getting the sum correct, (a subtraction sum of six figures). Tables & Mental Arith. was only "Fair"; some eight or nine children failed to correctly write a piece of Transcription; Reading taken as a whole was Good, as was also "The Horse" (Object Lesson.)
I am very disappointed with the result of the Examination, and I have expressed my disappointment to the Teacher (Miss. P. Boyer. Art 68)

7 A great drop in the attendance this afternoon, owing to many 1st Class boys going to see a Cricket Match. In consequence, I sent a circular letter, to the parents of the absent children.

Page from the log-book of the Royal British Schools. Who says illiteracy and truancy are modern trends? (DJ)

Academe

Only those of wealth and importance received education by right in the early 18th century. True, the Grammar Schools provided a medium whereby talented boys from humble circumstances could ascend the social ladder with their classical education, but the numbers achieving this were not great, and the period following the Civil War is often seen as one of decline for the Grammar Schools.

Thame was no exception to this rule, and Lord Williams's School slowly diminished in importance. The poor were excluded because of the fees and the rich and influential chose to patronise the larger schools or provided private tutors for their offspring instead. Headmasters of the School were more often than not clergymen holding down two jobs for financial reasons. With cures as far away as Chearsley, Long Crendon and Holton, the care of the dozen or so pupils suffered. By the time of Rev Lee (1814-1841), the Usher's post had been abolished and the salary appropriated to the Head—there were but 6 pupils in the School. The nadir was yet to come, but the decline of the Grammar School coincided with the energetic rise of other new educational establishments in the town.

These new schools basically fell into two categories: first, those which provided education of a classical or commercial nature, usually associated with boarding; second, those whose concern was the basic literacy of the working population. Many of these early private institutions were of an ephemeral nature, and can only be traced through chance mention in newspapers such as Jackson's *Oxford Journal.* Those which achieved a certain permanence include the Market House School, which had 54 pupils in 1833, part fee paying and part free; Mrs Way's Boarding School, mentioned in 1765; a girls' School run by Martha Bowler in 1768; and a Boarding School for girls established at North Weston Manor in 1819. The list could be extended *ad infinitum,* and some of these institutions were no doubt small and short-lived, yet they reflected the current opinion that the classical Grammar School curriculum was obsolete, and by providing an education for girls they were providing a service that the Grammar Schools had not even contemplated.

Of these private institutions, however, the most important and long-lived was the Howard House School, which began in 1840 in a house near Church Row. Its Headmaster, James Marsh, was an important figure in the locality, and the School expanded rapidly. There were 120 boarders and 30 day pupils in 1868, when the School amalgamated with another private venture, the Oxford County School (which had itself begun life 60 years earlier as the Mansion House School). The combined school operated in new central premises 'warmed by hot water apparatus' and educated children between the ages of 6 and 18. It gained a good reputation and was noted for the annual charity banquet given to the poor at Christmas. It ran into difficulties in the last years of the 19th century, and finally became a Preparatory School in 1900, and moved to London eight years later.

There was increasing pressure during the 19th century to extend the benefits of education to the labouring masses. The Churches took a leading role in this movement, which sprang from both genuine philanthropic motives and the idea that education would both train and control the masses in good habits. Schools therefore grew up erratically, according to local pressures and in many places like Thame the rivalry between Anglican and Dissenter was expressed in the establishment of rival institutions.

The first schools of this nature in Thame were either connected with charitable bequests (like the Market House School) or Sunday School. By 1833 Anglicans, Independents, Wesleyans, and Baptists all had schools of this nature. But the first major steps in this direction came with the establishment of two permanent denominational schools, named after the Religious Societies which promoted them. The National School (1838) was Anglican; whilst the Royal British and Foreign School (1837) was Nonconformist. Both were formed by subscription, and between them catered so well for the population of Thame that there was little need to supplement the provision in the town when the 1870 Education Act was passed, establishing nation-wide primary instruction.

The National School was situated in Hog Fair and was added to in 1842 when infants' premises were erected, and in 1900 when a new classroom was added. By then about 200 boys and girls attended. Fees of 2d to 6d a week were charged up to 1871. However, its fortunes wavered, and the reports of Inspectors were not always favourable. In 1929, the School transformed into a Senior (i.e. Secondary) School, and became the Secondary Modern in 1949. A new Secondary School (Wenman School) was built at the other end of the town, and the old National School buildings were demolished in September 1967.

The Royal British and Foreign Schools were erected in 1836 in Brick-kiln Lane. The poor were to be taught 'to apply their own ingenuity and industry'. Like its Anglican counterpart, it suffered several vicissitudes. Pupils and money declined badly in 1855, with the pupils absenting themselves at harvest time, and the buildings needed constant repair. Boarders were taken from 1850, and pupil teachers employed from 1867. Various extensions were made in 1852 and 1900 but numbers did not fluctuate that much; 220 in 1837, 186 in 1849, 256 in 1903. As Park Street School it transformed to become Thame's sole primary School in 1929. It is now known as the John Hampden School.

Both Moreton and Towersey had primary Schools as well, though the Thame Schools drew from quite a wide area. Moreton School lasted from 1860 to 1920 and

Towersey School from 1870 to 1958.

The education of girls in the town in the latter half of the 19th century was catered for by two big private Schools. Miss Todd's Academy took both boarders and day pupils but apparently did not survive beyond 1894. The other school, called Brunswick House School in 1872, was run by a Mrs Pearce, and by virtue of occupying the Tudor buildings of the Boys Grammar School (when Lord Williams's moved to Oxford Road) it became the Girls' Grammar School. In 1908 it moved again, this time to the buildings in the High Street vacated by the Oxford County School. It became the area Secondary School for girls, but boarders ceased in 1943 and amidst local furore it was closed in 1948, when the girls were accommodated at Wood Eaton whilst waiting for new accommodation at Wheatley. The building was shamefully demolished in 1965 for a projected chain store and has remained derelict until 1978, when signs of building activity began.

So education was very much a going concern in 19th century Thame, but the Boys' Grammar School was not part of this prosperity. Its decline was accentuated by the Headmastership of Rev T. Foolkes (1841-1879). The reverend gentleman seems to have had little vocation for teaching; he was noted for his harsh canings, and left the Usher to do most of the work. Not that there was much to do. By 1866, only two boys appeared on the School books and the playground was used for growing potatoes. The report of the Schools Inquiry Commission in 1869 was devastating. Only one pupil was in School and even his knowledge of reading, dictation and elementary arithmetic was 'bad'. Dr Foolkes tried to excuse this lamentable state of affairs by saying that the population of Thame was declining. But the Commissioner was not to be so easily deceived, for he was able to point to the thriving Howard House Academy nearby. A contemporary letter to the *Thame Gazette* described the School as 'a richly endowed but comparatively useless Institution' and one cannot but agree. Worse was to come; for a time (1870-1879) there were no pupils at all, the Headmaster having threatened to thrash any who turned up. Dr Foolkes found solace in the violin, away from the distractions of teaching.

A school without pupils must be unique in the story of education; but this state of affairs could not last for long. Dr Foolkes was forced to resign and received a handsome pension while New College took control and produced a new scheme of government. New buildings were proposed (one proposal involved demolition of the almshouses, but they were eventually sold instead), and a fresh site was acquired on the Oxford Road, and commodious buildings were erected in 1877-9, the architect being William Wilkinson of Oxford.

The new School commenced on 1 May 1879, under a new Headmaster, George Plummer, with 40 boys and 4 staff. Academic and sporting success soon followed, despite a sag in the numbers during the 1890s, partly due to a departing Headmaster in 1899 'poaching' 12 boarders away to his new School! Boarders were accommodated from the first, apparently under a somewhat strict regime. Parents were informed that pupils were not to have 'private stores of food and luxuries' (apart from one hamper a term—liquor being specifically forbidden) or trouser pockets, which were designated as 'great snares to indolent boys', especially for those 'inclined to be round-shouldered, or to avoid games'.

The School became a voluntary controlled establishment in 1944, but the greatest changes have been in recent years. In 1972, it merged with the Wenman Secondary School to form the split-site Lord Williams Comprehensive School, the Oxford Road site being used for the 14-18 age range. In 1975, a second Lower School was built adjacent to the Upper School. Total numbers in 1978 exceed 2,100, making it one of the largest Schools in the country. Lord Williams might well feel bemused by the present size and curriculum of the School that bears his name.

To complete the educational story of Thame in the 1970s a new Primary School has been built at Barley Hill to serve the new estates, and a Roman Catholic Primary School erected near the Catholic Church. In addition, from 1938, the old Workhouse building has been occupied by Rycotewood College, providing instruction in a wide range of craft skills. New buildings were added in 1939, and the town has perhaps regained some of the educational fame it enjoyed in the 16th and 17th centuries.

Two views of the John Hampden School, built as the Royal British Schools in 1836.

ABOVE: John Hampden School and Park Street in more leisured days.
BELOW: Barley Hill, Thame's second primary school. (QPS)

School-children at play in a deserted Chinnor Road at the turn of the century.

A class in gymnastic pose outside the Grammar School early this century.

OPPOSITE: A poster of Oxford County School, about 1900.

EDUCATION FOR SONS OF GENTLEMEN.

PARENTS AND GUARDIANS ARE INFORMED THAT THE

Oxford County School,

THAME,

OF WHICH IS HEAD MASTER

THOMAS GARDNER,

ASSISTED BY RESIDENT MASTERS,

RECEIVES A LIMITED NUMBER OF PUPILS TO EDUCATE & PREPARE FOR THE UNIVERSITIES,

COMPETITIVE EXAMINATIONS,

PROFESSIONAL AND MERCANTILE PURSUITS.

EVERY ATTENTION IS PAID TO THE MENTAL, MORAL, AND RELIGIOUS CULTURE OF EACH PUPIL.

THOROUGH TEACHING, NOT CRAMMING, KIND TREATMENT WITH CAREFUL SUPERVISION.

Oxford County School is beautifully and healthily situated surrounded by extensive recreation grounds.
The air is mild and salubrious, while the outstretching country affords pleasant walks.

CRICKET, FOOTBALL, AND GYMNASIUM PRACTICE.

PROSPECTUS & TESTIMONIALS ON APPLICATION.

ABOVE: Front view of the Girls' Grammar School, formerly the Oxford County School. The building was allowed to decay and eventually demolished. CENTRE: Side view of the rear buildings of the school. BELOW: Rear view of the school.

ABOVE: Cuttlebrook House, once a school, latterly a book-shop, and now a private residence. (QPS) BELOW: A front view of the Oxford County School in the 19th Century.

Views of the Oxford County School. ABOVE: the Bath and Gym.
CENTRE: the Entrance Hall. BELOW: the Dining Hall. OPPOSITE:
interior views of the Bath and Gym.

ABOVE: The old Grammar School, as it was in 1883. BELOW: The new
Grammar School on the Oxford Road, as newly built.

ABOVE: Cricket in a bleak landscape outside the school. The building to the left is possibly the old toll-gate. CENTRE and BELOW: From the printed advertisement sheet for Lord Williams's, early this century, issued by the Headmaster, Dr A. E. Shaw.

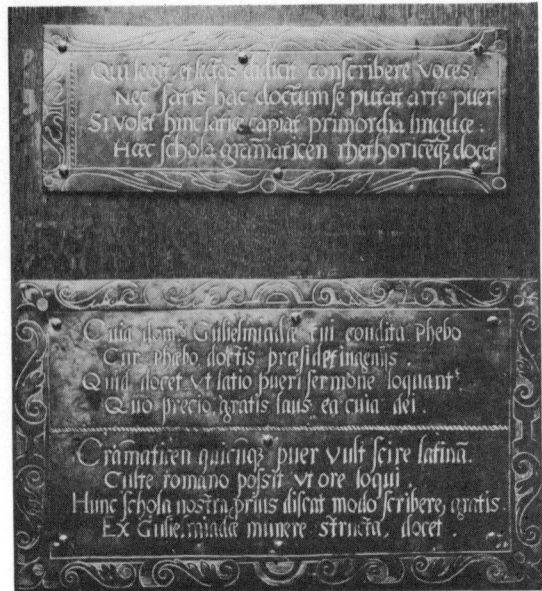

ABOVE LEFT: Brasses, formerly in the Old Grammar School, now in the Boarders' Refectory. RIGHT: A copy of the School Statutes. Originally the master had to have a copy bolted onto his desk, so that he always taught 'on the statutes'. BELOW: Overhead view of Lord Williams's School, before the major additions of recent years.

Feby 11. 1865 —

Gentlemen

Having been for a long time intimately acquainted with Mr Percival Field, both as a pupil of the school, over which I preside, and also as a friend & neighbour; I have much pleasure in giving my testimony to his character for steadiness, activity, intelligence, & integrity. I have perfect confidence that in any employment he will be found diligent & thoroughly trust-worthy

T. B. Fookes D. C. L
Head Master. Thame Grammar School

Testimonial from Dr Fookes, Headmaster in 1865, for Percy Field, whom he had thrashed unmercifully and expelled in 1860. By contrast, the letter is warm in tone.

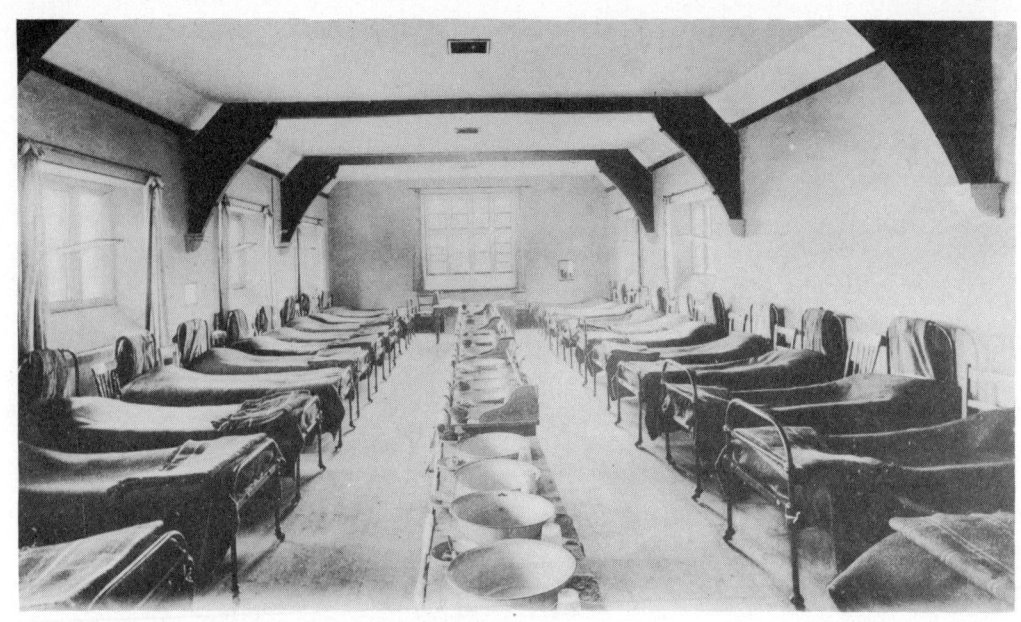

ABOVE: Dormitory accommodation in the Boarding House in the 1920s.
BELOW: Rev T. T. Lee, vicar of Thame and Headmaster 1814-41. There
were 'rarely more than six boys in the foundation at one time' whilst he
was in charge.

In The Public Interest

The idea that society as a whole bore a responsibility for the welfare of its citizens was one that grew slowly over the ages. A static, family-based society was perhaps able to cope with its social problems. The best the poor of the Middle Ages could hope for was a haphazard system. Churchwardens occasionally doled out to deserving cases. A 'poor man that died at Hew Fullers' in 1549 was donated a shroud, whilst Elizabeth Way received a handout two years later when 'her house was visited with the Plague'. The poor were sometimes given free beer at Easter, but otherwise they might well have to fall back on charity, and hence the importance of bequests such as that of Richard Quatremains in 1448, who founded an almshouse for six poor men. The request was augmented by Lord Williams, partly out of the funds of the dissolved Quatremains guild.

At best this sort of system only scraped the surface of the problem: at worst, the poor and destitute were driven to vagrancy and crime. It was this concern for social control which led to the first systematic attempts at poor relief under Queen Elizabeth. 'Sturdy Beggars' were to be whipped for their pains, but the deserving 'impotent poor' were to be relieved by parochial rates. Thame's earliest rate book shows about 80 ratepayers contributing a total of about 35s a month for the relief of about 30 paupers.

However, the fear that the poor might lose the urge to work if they were over-pampered lay deep in the hearts of the administrators of the Poor Law. The County House of Correction was built in 1720 to employ the able-bodied poor. The system was cheaper than out-relief (i.e. direct payments to paupers), but subject to abuse. The Keeper of the House apparently kept well away, in Aylesbury, and his assistant found that keeping lodgers was more palatable than supervising the poor. Later it became the custom to 'contract out' the supervision of the Workhouse to the highest bidder. In 1776 a measure of order was restored with the drawing up of regulations of conduct for the Workhouse, but it was still clearly a commercial venture, for he was to retain the profits of work done in the House. The Workhouse moved to the former bridewell in 1790 (the site of the Jolly Sailor)—a symbolic move this, for poverty was often regarded as a form of crime. Thame's system of law and order at this time consisted of a single Constable and pair of stocks, reinforced by the Justices at Quarter Sessions in Oxford. There was a fair spectrum of crime, as reported in Jackson's *Oxford Journal*. Footpads and highwaymen lurked by the roadsides.

Their fate, if caught, would probably have been the gallows, like the murderer from Tetsworth in 1785 who was executed at Milton Common in chains in front of an alleged crowd of 20,000. On a less exalted note, two men were condemned to death in 1766 for stealing 6 cows in Thame. Three years earlier female felons had been branded on their hands. The most frequent crimes, however, seem to have been poaching (especially in Thame Park) and drunkenness — hardly surprising in view of the large number of Inns and Ale-houses in the area.

Lord Torrington, when he visited Thame in 1785, described it as a 'mean, gloomy town'. His Lordship's proverbial melancholy was perhaps in some sense justified. For 18th century Thame was agricultural and provincial, perhaps even parochial, to a large degree. The tidal waves of the outside world rippled into this static, stable and self-centred society, only slowly. To the casual visitor, the vast emptiness of the High Street and the grandeur of the splendid brick houses flanking the sides must have been impressive, but the unhealthy and insanitary condition of the streets must .have detracted from the picture. There were, of course, regulations concerning public health, and the Court of Frankpledge enforced the actions of the Scavengers in keeping the streets clean (every ten days!). Yet some of the decisions are revealing; individuals had the responsibility for repairs to the water supply and gutters in the street; dunghills were supposed not to remain in the streets for more than 10 days; no garbage or entrails were to be thrown into the street. The fact that such regulations existed is sure proof of these things happening. No wonder infectious disease claimed so many lives in England two hundred years ago.

The reluctance for authorities to act in the public interest was partly financial and partly ideological. More 'interference' in matters such as health and poverty would have meant increased local rates, as fiercely contested then as now. However, it was also felt that authorities had no right to act in these areas; this *laissez-faire* protected the individual against the busy-bodying encroachments of governments and other authorities. However, these views came under attack during the 19th century as the size of the problems increased under the pressures of urban growth. Thame dutifully followed in the van of these developments, and it is time now to examine these local affairs.

First, the poor. There was a vast expansion in the numbers needing relief at the turn of the century, as war abroad and poor harvests added to the usual crop of paupers. To avert catastrophic starvations, relief was index-linked to the price of corn in 1795. But this led to abuses by employers and workmen alike, and the decision to establish a country-wide system of Workhouses in 1834 was intended to encourage both economies and changed attitudes. Groups of parishes were formed into 'Unions', each with a Central Workhouse. In Thame, the Institution was built in 1836-7 on a site at Priestend. The Union served 35 parishes, stretching as far as Brill to the East and Lewknor to the West.

Workhouses were to be 'safety nets' to deal with the deserving poor in a humane and efficient manner, but to prevent malingering, facilities in workhouses were kept Spartan, and the inmates subjected to work and discipline. Thame Workhouse was to accommodate 350 men and women, but under pressure in the 1840s, extensions were made to receive another 60. The buildings, by Wilkinson of Witney, were of a standard plan; men, women and children were kept separate. Apart from domestic and work areas, the paupers had only the dormitories to live in. A master and his wife (who acted as matron) were appointed, along with school teachers for the pauper children, and a Porter for the gate; all came under the fastidious charge of an elected Board of Guardians. In addition, a doctor and chaplain were appointed to attend to the physical and spiritual welfare of the inmates.

The Workhouse was generally despised by those forced to patronise it, but many were scarcely in the position to criticise it, as the alternatives were bleak. As an omnibus institution, Thame's Workhouse had to deal with all facets of distressed humanity: the poor, the elderly, orphans and bastards, the deprived and the depraved. The Minute Books of the Guardians give a fair impression of the regime. Paupers did not have to wear a uniform, though suitable clothes were provided, but barbers were regularly contracted for 'shaving' at 10d per dozen. Menial work was provided for able-bodied men from 1841 (and any women not needed for domestic chores), unpicking oakum, a thick rope substance (they also tried rough cocao mat fibre in 1840). Bone crushing (for fertiliser) was also tried for a period from 1843, but this was forbidden by the Poor Law Commissioners in London in 1845, following the notorious scandal at Andover, when ravenous paupers gnawed the marrow from their day's pile. Children were educated in the Workhouse School, and kept away from adults. Discipline varied with the teachers; in 1846, the Schoolmaster was carpeted for drunkenness and absence, and an air of 'General Insubordination' prevailed in the School. On the other hand, corporal punishment of the children was expressly forbidden by the Guardians. In 1862 'drums and fifes . . . and other amusements' were presented to the boys.

Discipline was a major problem in the Thame Workhouse, it seems, especially in the Vagrant Ward. As they were not usually *bona fide* paupers, the vagrants were consigned to an outside barn and expected to put in a morning's hard labour. Predictably several refused, and had to be taken to the Magistrates. Others found a novel way of exploiting the charity provided; they tore their old clothes on arrival, forcing the Workhouse to re-equip them. Vagrant numbers grew steadily over the years. 961 cases were relieved in 1844, but by 1847 the number had risen to 2,790. Some of the permanent residents were also recalcitrant: one pauper was put in a week's isolation on a bread and water diet in 1841 for throwing snowballs at the Master! Absenteeism in town (and in the women's ward) also occurred quite frequently, and in an extreme case in 1847 a man was flogged for absconding with Workhouse property. But on the other hand the regime was fair. The complaints of paupers (and other interested outsiders) were fully investigated, and a couple of Porters dismissed for unsuitability. The health of the paupers was carefully monitored—a complaint of a 'lousy bed' (literally) was investigated carefully;

Thame Union.

Extract from the QUARTERLY ABSTRACT, shewing the number of Paupers relieved, the am[…] due to and from the several Parishes, for the Quarter ending Chr[…]

Schedule B.—Form 11a.

PARISHES.	Population.	Acreage.	Average of Rates for three years, to 5th March, 1839. £.	TOTALS. In-door. Adults. Males.	In-door. Adults. Females.	In-door. Children.	Out-door. Adults. Males.	Out-door. Adults. Females.	Out-door. Children.	GRAND TOTAL.	Repayment of Workhouse Loan. £. s. d.	In-Maintenance. £.	s.	d.	Out-Relief. £.	s.	d.	Proportion of Establishment Charges. £.	s.	d.	Total Expe[…] for the r[…] the P[…] £.
North District.																					
1 ALBURY	244	550	48	..	..	..	3	3	2	8	....	..	..	..	11	9	1	2	18	0	14
2 BRILL	1449	2600	626	21	12	15	60	80	115	303	....	27	14	7	233	1	3¾	37	16	0	298
3 CHILTON	364	2080	262	6	2	3	15	23	20	69	....	12	6	2	66	6	9½	15	16	5	94
4 DORTON	151	890	74	..	1	6	3	10	13	33	....	7	2	0	26	10	9½	4	9	4	38
5 ICKFORD	386	1205	99	5	3	3	13	10	9	43	....	2	3	11	30	9	8½	5	19	6	38
6 LONG CRENDON	1656	3350	828	14	6	13	42	77	56	208	....	24	2	4	193	0	5½	49	18	0	367
7 OAKLEY	391	2250	178	2	2	2	11	24	17	58	....	1	5	11	64	6	2¾	10	14	9	76
8 SHABBINGTON	366	1880	198	6	8	17	18	28	17	94	....	22	2	4	81	3	4½	11	19	0	115
9 TIDDINGTON	198	700	70	2	1	5	..	4	..	12	....	2	4	2	7	10	5	4	4	5	13
10 THOMLEY	270	640	21	..	..	..	..	..	..	..	....	..	..	..	..	..	..	1	5	3	1
11 WATERPERRY		1930	146	1	3	5	7	10	14	40	....	11	19	10	29	18	8½	8	16	3	50
12 WATERSTOCK	127	660	50	..	..	..	3	5	6	14	....	..	..	..	14	1	5	3	0	3	17
13 WORMINGHALL	314	1360	69	6	1	..	13	11	14	45	....	3	12	4	35	10	11	4	3	3	43
Thame District.																					
14 ASTON ROWANT	946	2980	533	6	4	8	35	56	40	149	....	9	4	10	141	11	9¼	32	3	1	182
15 CROWELL	167	116	134	3	..	1	9	11	6	30	....	6	4	7	21	10	9	8	1	9	38
16 EMMINGTON	97	750	39	..	..	..	2	5	4	11	....	..	..	..	10	3	10½	2	7	0	12
17 KINGSEY	237	1350	114	..	3	6	9	14	18	50	....	4	16	3	38	7	3½	6	17	7	50
18 SYDENHAM	438	1500	258	14	6	18	12	25	23	98	....	15	2	4	49	10	9	15	11	7	80
19 TETSWORTH	523	840	280	3	1	7	21	27	40	99	....	12	7	6	[illegible]	5	2¼	13	17	9	103
20 THAME	3060	5100	1629	43	23	58	79	164	111	478	....	113	7	2½	378	14	1½	98	4	2	590
South District.																					
21 ADWELL	46	500	25	..	..	..	1	2	2	5	....	..	..	..	3	5	2	1	10	2	4
22 ASCOTT	97	576	55	..	..	..	..	..	..	..	....	..	..	..	..	..	..	3	6	3	3
23 CHILWORTH	..	1077	75	..	3	3	10	9	1	26	....	7	6	0	39	8	6½	4	10	5	42
24 CHARLGROVE	691	2120	430	1	3	5	21	33	17	80	....	10	5	0	100	19	2¾	25	19	1	137
25 EASINGTON	24	380	1	..	..	..	1	1	..	2	....	..	..	..	2	1	0	0	1	2½	2
26 GREAT HASELEY	764	3219	488	14	6	3	31	53	38	145	....	9	16	1	128	0	9¾	29	9	1	167
27 GREAT MILTON	737	1399	188	2	2	2	18	26	24	74	....	7	19	10	73	6	7¼	11	7	0	92
28 LITTLE MILTON	482	1351	243	7	..	..	15	24	21	67	....	4	5	5	69	16	2	14	13	3	88
29 LEWKNOR	847	4690	333	3	7	7	27	31	20	95	....	18	3	0	113	4	9	20	2	0	151
30 LEWKNOR UPHILL			162	1	..	..	12	21	17	51	....	1	13	0	55	12	6¼	9	15	7	67
31 SHIRBURN	338	2230	237	1	3	2	18	32	22	78	....	2	10	11	79	11	4	14	6	0	96
32 SOUTH WESTON	104	570	37	1	..	..	2	3	..	6	....	1	13	0	10	1	0	2	4	7	13
33 STOKE TALMAGE	101	720	54	..	1	1	5	7	10	24	....	3	6	0	25	6	1	3	5	2	31
34 WARPSGROVE	23	333	21	..	1	..	2	1	3	7	....	0	1	8	5	2	1	1	5	3	6
35 WHEATFIELD	99	540	86	..	1	..	4	9	10	24	....	1	13	0	26	11	8¾	5	3	8	33
TOTAL..	15739	52436	8041	162	103	190	522	839	710	2526	....	344	9	[illegible]	2236	19	11¾	485	2	0½	3066
As compared with the corresponding Quarter of last Year. Increase				..	..	..	23	3	..	..	....	..	..	..	73	0	0¼	119	4	3¾	167
Diminution				61	7	17	..	..	29	88	....	24	11	[illegible]	..	..	..	..	..	..	..

OFFICERS ON SERVICE IN THE UNION.				
NAME.	OFFICE.	Salary per annum. £.	s.	d.
John Hollier	Clerk	100	0	0
Richard Holloway	Auditor	20	0	0
Thomas Stone	Treasurer	0	0	0
Rev. Amos Hayton	Chaplain	40	0	0
Wm. Simmons	Master	75	0	0
Maria C. Simmons	Matron	35	0	0
John Jonas Shrimpton	Relieving Officer	57	15	0
Eden White	Same	57	15	0
Thomas Home	Same	57	15	0
William Jaques	Schoolmaster	25	0	0
Harriet Lester	Schoolmistress	20	0	0
George Painter	Porter	25	0	0

CONTRACT PRICES, DURING THE QUARTER, OF PROVISIONS AND OTHER ARTICLES USED IN THE UNION.													
	Bread.	Meat.	Butter.	Cheese.	Potatoes.	Peas.	Oatmeal.	Candles.	Soap.	Coals.	Flour.	Milk.	Su[…]
Description...	Best Seconds	Beef and Mutton.	Best Irish,	Flat Dutch,		Split,	Best,	Best dips,	Yellow,	Best Moira,	Best Seconds,	New,	R[…]
Price	at 5d. per 4lb. loaf.	at 5s. 6d. per stone.	at 70s. 0d. per cwt.	at 42s. 0d. per cwt.	at 1s. 6d. per cwt.	at 7s. 9d. per bushel.	at 14s. 0d. per cwt.	at 6s. 6d. per doz.	[illegible] per cwt.	at 26s. 6d. per ton.	at 37s. per sack.	at 8d. per gall.	at 5[…] per[…]

Examined with the Q[…]

pended, and the Balances

[ROBSON, PRINTER, THAME.]

cination Fees.		Total Expenditure, including Relief to the Poor, Registration and Vaccination Fees.			Balance due to the Parish.			Balance due from the Parish.			
s.	d.	£.	s.	d.	£.	s.	d.	£.	s.	d.	
..	..	14	7	1	..	..	..	1	0	10½	1
..	..	299	19	10¾	..	..	..	70	8	1	2
..	..	94	19	4½	..	..	..	15	11	6	3
..	..	38	5	1½	..	..	..	4	17	3¾	4
..	..	38	19	7½	..	..	..	2	16	7¾	5
..	..	268	15	3½	10	17	11	..	..	..	6
..	..	77	3	4¾	14	18	9¼	..	..	..	7
..	..	115	12	2½	..	..	..	3	18	8½	8
..	..	14	1	0	9	2	7	..	..	..	9
..	..	1	5	3	0	6	5¼	..	..	..	10
..	..	51	0	9½	..	..	..	2	4	0½	11
..	..	17	4	2	2	2	11¾	..	..	..	12
..	..	43	11	0	..	..	..	3	18	1½	13
9	0	183	17	8¼	25	8	5¼	..	..	..	14
..	..	38	17	7	6	12	10	..	..	..	15
..	..	12	18	4½	1	13	10	..	..	..	16
..	..	50	3	7½	2	3	1½	..	..	..	17
..	..	80	17	2	12	17	2	..	..	..	18
..	..	104	3	5¼	5	14	2¼	..	..	..	19
..	..	592	15	0	120	7	2½	..	..	..	20
..	..	4	15	4	4	1	5	..	..	..	21
..	..	3	6	3	2	8	10¾	..	..	..	22
..	..	42	8	5½	14	19	3	..	..	..	23
..	..	138	2	9¾	24	2	5¾	..	..	..	24
..	..	2	2	2½	..	..	..	1	7	5½	25
..	..	168	5	11¾	43	12	10	..	..	..	26
..	..	93	6	5¼	4	2	11¼	..	..	..	27
..	..	88	19	10	9	8	5¾	..	..	..	28
..	..	152	7	9	..	..	..	21	0	8¼	29
..	..	67	2	1¼	..	..	..	12	14	7½	30
..	..	96	15	3	..	..	..	1	10	1¾	31
..	..	14	3	1	..	..	..	6	5	9¾	32
..	..	31	17	3	..	..	..	3	2	7¾	33
..	..	6	12	6	..	..	..	2	5	1¾	34
..	..	33	8	4¾	..	..	..	2	3	1½	35
9	0	3082	10	8¾	315	1	9¼	155	4	11¼	
9	0	168	2	7¾	..	..	..	..	..	..	
..	..	..	..	..	..	..	..	..	..	..	

MEDICAL OFFICERS.

	£.		£.
S KNIGHT, *Brill*	60	JOHN STONE, *Watlington*	60
W. REYNOLDS, *Thame*	75	Dr. AYRES, *Thame*	45
LLE LUPTON, *Thame*	80	JOHN SMITH, *Wheatley*	10
S STEVENS, *Great Milton*	45	RICHARD LEE, *Thame*	45
. KIMPTON, *Stadhampton*	36		

RELIEVING OFFICERS.

orth District.	Thame District.	South District.
ONAS SHRIMPTON, ONG CRENDON.	EDEN WHITE, THAME.	THOMAS HOME, GREAT HASELEY.

t, Jno Hollier, Clerk.

LEFT: Notice of Poor Law expenditure by the parishes constituting the Thame Union. (OCRO)

admissions were stopped in 1843 when smallpox was detected. Vaccination certificates were widely issued. Food contractors were rigorously pursued if their products fell below acceptable standards. Charity usually prevailed at Christmas, when a feast was provided for the children and old people, consisting of beef, plum pudding, bread and a pint of beer for the men.

A glance at the table will demonstrate the bare statistics of the Workhouse population in 1851. The figures are notable for the relative lack of aged poor (perhaps they just didn't survive, or were cared for by their children) and the high number of middle-aged and children resident. However, the number *resident* is but the tip of the iceberg, for the Guardians also dispensed out-relief in cases of temporary distress, or where Workhouse accommodation was unsuitable or unavailable. The Thame Union was divided into 3 areas, each with its own Medical and Relieving Officers, who had the job of assessing the merits of claimants for relief. All cases were charged to the parish of origin, but in some cases an 'order of filiation' could be made through the courts to force the fathers of illegitimate offspring to meet some of their obligations. In some cases, the parishes dragged their feet in payment and were prosecuted. But poor relief could be an expensive item, especially when the Guardians were prepared to sanction funds to aid emigrations to Canada and Australia.

Nevertheless, reliance on 'The Parish' was obnoxious to most, and agricultural fluctuations meant severe hardship for many labourers, who were therefore doubtless grateful for further charity. Lady Wenman of Thame Park was especially bountiful, donating for example 18 tons of coal, 1,200 lb of prime beef, 800 yards of flannel and 36 jerseys in 1863. There were annual collections for coal for the poor at this time. Many of the older charities continued to function. In 1820, for example, Burrowe's and Robotham's charities were yielding 20 gowns per annum. Funge's charity provided 30 3d loaves weekly; Hart's Charity financed an apprentice; another charity provided for the Widow's Groat (4d) at Christmas. Many of these charities were dispensed from the 'poor stone'—the Quatremains tomb in the Parish Church.

The Charities still exist, though in a revised form since 1977, when they were reorganised as the Thame Welfare Trust. The sum of £622 was distributed out of the Charities funds in 1977. The Almsmen of Lord Williams are also still appointed; though since 1880 they have been no longer resident in the almshouse, and are no longer required to wear uniform. The six recipients in 1978 were receiving 63p a week.

The centralised authority of the Poor Law Guardians provided the example for other areas of public concern in the 19th century. Thame did not adopt the Local Government Act of 1858 until 1871. From that date, an elected local Board of Health operated, which subsumed all matters of health, road maintenance, and sanitation. By all accounts this body had plenty to contend with. Smallpox had visited Thame in 1843 and 1865, and scarletina in 1871 (killing 16 people) and the *Thame Gazette* contained advertisements for patent cholera mixtures. The report of the investigating Medical Officer, Dr Buchanan, was devastating. Not only was there no place to put the infected sick; the causes of the problem were plain to see. In High Street 'there run open gutters, which receive all manner of liquid house slop and other filth, probably the washings of certain slaughter-houses in the middle of the town'. 'These gutters are roughly constructed and have but a slow stream along them. The gutters enter various ditches, most of which are nearly stagnant.' At Cuttle-Brook was a ditch whose contents included 'fellmongers slops', to the left 'an expanse of black mud', to the right a ditch 'draining an establishment in which offal is boiled down and pigs fed thereon'. The crowning foulness was that the driver of a cart was ladling this 'sewage' into barrels for use in 'a certain brewery' to be 'converted into beer'.

Local medical opinion was not totally in accord with this Chamber of Horrors, but Dr Lee was able to confirm that a cesspool in the town was only 8 feet from a well. Once the Board was established, some progress was made. Proper gutters were laid in 1874, and enforcement notices were served to control 'nuisances' in the streets. It was in fact not until 1900 that proper sewage pumping machinery was installed, and that has been replaced twice since. But the root cause of the evil, the water supply, was not tackled properly until late in the day, and infectious disease continued to plague the town until well into the 20th century; in 1905 the system of about 150 wells was by supplies obtained by drillings near Towersey. Extra works were completed in 1946.

One service that gained immediately from these improvements was the fire brigade. A fire engine was acquired by public subscription in 1817—and a new one produced in 1870 (from Merryweather and Sons), which pumped 130 gallons per minute, but the Thame volunteer brigade could not always provide adequate cover. In 1874, at a fire at Thame Park, there was confusion because the Thame Brigade wore no uniform, and a shake-up took place in 1878 when the Brigade came under the charge of the Town Surveyor and a new engine house built near Whitehound Pond. A new fire station was built in Nelson Street in 1937.

Richard Quatremains founded a 'hospital' in Thame in the 15th century, (which probably means accommodation for the elderly), which was subsumed by Lord Williams's Almshouses. Such medical help as existed between the Reformation and the 19th century was probably provided by individual doctors, surgeons and apothecaries. From 1834, their work was channelled more towards the poor through the New Poor Law, and county asylums were established for the insane. Thame lacked a hospital until 1898, when the present Cottage Hospital in East Street was built as a Nursing Home, thus obviating the necessity to journey to the Radcliffe Infirmary in Oxford. There have been several subsequent extensions and improvements. However, the prolification of patent medical advertisements in the *Thame Gazette* of the last century suggests many preferred recourse to private remedies.

Some of the functions of the Old Parish Constables were thus absorbed by new authorities, but this cannot have made their job much easier. From 1852, they were supervised from Wheatley, and in 1854 a police station was built. Prior to that, prisoners had to be taken to Oxford, or detained in the Constable's own house. A report of 1857 even alleged that the Thame Constabulary dumped vagrants over the Bucks border to be rid of the bother of them. The present County Court was built in 1861. Now, in 1978, the police station may be on the move again; the site is not yet certain.

Thus, by slow and cumbersome stages, Thame developed ways of regulating and dealing with the social welfare of its inhabitants, a process greatly speeded up by the establishment of Urban District Councils in 1894, and the development of County-based agencies this century.

The Birdcage Inn, jail for Napoleonic prisoners, as it was in the 1950s.

92

The Police Station, as built.

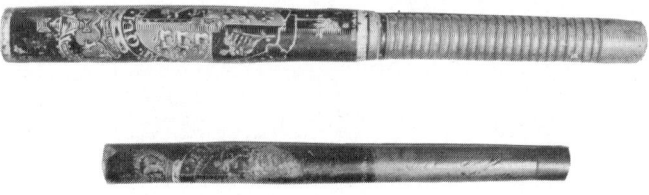

Constable's truncheons from Thame (Ash. M)

ABOVE: The Jolly Sailor, site of the former Bridewell. BELOW: The almshouses of Lord Williams. Though no longer serving their original purpose, they make an attractive grouping with the old Grammar School.

Age Group	Males Total in Group		Females Total in Group
Over 70	8		2
61 - 70	15		5
51 - 60	9		3
41 - 50	8		6
31 - 40	7		7
21 - 30	11		22
11 - 20	20		19
0 - 10	32		28
Total	110	Total in Workhouse 202	Total 92

ABOVE: View of the former Workhouse, before recent additions were made. BELOW: An analysis of Workhouse inmates in 1851.

95

To the Guardians

of the Poor of the *Thame* Union,
in the Count*ies* of *Oxford and Bucks*

and to all others, whom it may concern.

Know all Men by these Presents,

A Messuage Homestead Garden and Close in Priestend in the Parish of Thame containing 7-3-18 including the Site of the Buildings belonging to the Earl of Abingdon held by John Jemmett by Copy of Court Roll of the Manor of Priestend for the life of one George Preacher.— And 4-3-12 of Freehold Land in Priestend aforesaid adjoining the first mentioned Premises the Property of the Right Honorable Sophia Elizabeth Baroness Wenman being part of a Close called the Parsonage Close as the same is now marked out and Parcel of the Thame Prebendal Estate.—

That, WE, The Poor Law Commissioners for England and Wales, by and with the consent of a Majority of the Guardians of the said Union, testified in Writing at the foot of a Duplicate of these Presents, and in pursuance of the powers given to us in and by an Act passed in the Fourth and Fifth Years of the Reign of His present Majesty King William the Fourth, intituled " *An Act for the* " *Amendment and better Administration of the Laws relating* " *to the Poor in England and Wales,*" do, by this Instrument under our Hands and Seal, ORDER and DIRECT—

First.—That the Guardians of the said Union shall purchase of the Owner or Owners of the same, the piece or parcel of Land described in the Margin hereof at or for a Sum not exceeding *Five hundred and Ninety Pounds*

Secondly.—That such piece of Land shall be conveyed by proper Assurances to the Guardians of the said Union and their successors, and shall be appropriated when so conveyed to the purpose of Building the Workhouse hereinafter ordered to be built, and for such other purposes relating to the Relief of the Poor of the said Union, as the said Guardians shall direct.

Thirdly.—That the Guardians of the said Union shall within Twelve Calendar Months from the date hereof, build, or cause to be built, upon the said piece of Land hereinbefore ordered to be purchased, a Workhouse for the common use of the several Parishes of the said Union, and that such Workhouse shall be of a size sufficient to hold *three hundred and fifty* Persons, Men, Women, and Children, properly classified, and shall be built according to such Plan as we shall approve (such approval to be testified by some writing under our Hands and Seal), subject never-

The official notice to establish a workhouse in Thame. (OCRO)

THAME UNION.

TO THE GUARDIANS of the POOR of the THAME UNION, *in the Counties of Oxford and Buckingham;---To the Clerk or Clerks to the Justices of Petty Sessions, held for the Division or Divisions of Petty Sessions of the said Counties in which the Parishes and Places comprised in the said Union are situate;---and to all others whom it may concern.*

WE, THE POOR LAW COMMISSIONERS FOR ENGLAND and WALES, in pursuance of the Provisions of an Act passed in the fourth and fifth Years of the Reign of HIS PRESENT MAJESTY KING WILLIAM THE FOURTH, intituled "*An Act for the Amendment and better Administration of the Laws relating to the Poor in ENGLAND and WALES,*" do hereby ORDER AND DIRECT that the Paupers of the respective Classes and Sexes described in the Schedule hereunto annexed, who may now or hereafter be received and maintained in the Workhouse or Workhouses of the THAME UNION, shall, during the period of their residence therein, be fed, dieted, and maintained with the food and in the manner described and set forth in the said Schedule.

AND WE DO HEREBY FURTHER ORDER AND DIRECT, that every Master of the Workhouse or Workhouses of the said Union, shall cause two or more Copies of this our Order and of the said Schedule, printed in a legible manner and in a large type, to be hung up in the most Public Places of such Workhouse or Workhouses, and to renew the same from time to time, so that it be always kept fair and legible, on pain of incurring, in case of disobedience, the Penalties provided by the aforesaid Act.

Given under our Hands and Seal, this eighteenth day of November, in the Year One Thousand Eight Hundred and Thirty-six.

SEAL OF THE POOR LAW COMMISSIONERS FOR ENGLAND & WALES

T. FRANKLAND LEWIS.

J. G. S. LEFEVRE.

GEO. NICHOLLS.

Dietary for able bodied Men and Women.

		Breakfast.		Dinner.					Supper.*		
		Bread.	Gruel.	Bread.	Cooked Meat.	Potatoes.	Soup.	Suet or rice Pudding.	Bread.	Cheese.	Gruel or Broth.
		oz.	Pints.	oz.	oz.	lb.	Pints.	oz.	oz.	oz.	Pints.
SUNDAY	Men	6	1½	4	5	½	–	–	6	–	1½
	Women	5	1½	3	5	½	–	–	5	–	1½
MONDAY	Men	6	1½	4	–	–	1½	–	6	1	–
	Women	5	1½	3	–	–	1½	–	5	1	–
TUESDAY	Men	6	1½	4	–	–	1½	–	6	–	1½
	Women	5	1½	3	–	–	1½	–	5	–	1½
WEDNESDAY	Men	6	1½	4	–	–	1½	–	6	1	–
	Women	5	1½	3	–	–	1½	–	5	1	–
THURSDAY	Men	6	1½	4	5	½	–	–	6	–	1½
	Women	5	1½	3	5	½	–	–	5	–	1½
FRIDAY	Men	6	1½	–	–	–	–	14	6	–	1½
	Women	5	1½	–	–	–	–	12	5	–	1½
SATURDAY	Men	6	1½	4	–	–	1½	–	6	1	–
	Women	5	1½	3	–	–	1½	–	5	1	–

OLD PEOPLE, of 60 years of age, and upwards may be allowed 1oz. of Tea, 5oz. of Butter, and 7oz. of Sugar per week, in lieu of Gruel for Breakfast, if deemed expedient to make this change.

CHILDREN, under 9 years of age, to be dieted at discretion, above 9 to be allowed the same quantities as Women.

SICK to be dieted as directed by the Medical Officer.

**SUPPER---The Gruel or Broth may be substituted for the Cheese, and vice versa.*

H. BRADFORD, PRINTER, THAME.

The Thame Pauper's dietary. Every pauper in the workhouse had the right to demand that his rations be weighed out in front of him. (OCRO)

Prior Joseph 22 Single Medical &
extras allowed

"

Stoke Talmage Jones James 37 Wife 32 and 5
Children Nurse & 2/. & 1 loaf allowed
for Wife

"

Chilton Edwards David 36 Wife 34 and 6
Children allowed 6/6 and 10 loaves
during illness

"

Long Crendon Wyatt John 35 Wife 30 & 3
Children allowed 1/6 in kind two
weeks to Wife confined
Archer Rich.d 27 Wife 28 & 1 Child allow'd
2/6 & 3 loaves during Childs illness

"

Crowell Hill David 30 Wife 29 allowed 5/ in
kind for one week

"

Towersey Williams Solomon 33 Wife 31 & 7
Children allowed 2/6 in kind two
weeks to Wife confined
Thame Moreton Henry 35 Wife 30 and
Children al   5/6 and 5
during

Page from the Guardians' Minute Book. The cases of individual paupers
for out-relief were being examined.

OPPOSITE:
A full list of officials and officers of the Thame Union Workhouse, 1839.

THAME UNION.

GUARDIANS AND OFFICERS, 1839.

CHARLES JOHN BAILLIE HAMILTON, Esq., Chairman.
The Rev. EDWARD FANSHAWE GLANVILLE, Vice Chairman.

Ex Officio Guardians.

The Earl of MACCLESFIELD, *Shirburn Castle.*
The Hon. and Rev. FREDERICK BERTIE, *Albury.*
Sir HENRY JOHN LAMBERT, Bart., *Aston Rowant.*
WILLIAM HENRY ASHHURST, Esq., *Waterstock.*
WILLIAM HENRY ASHHURST, Jun., Esq., *Waterstock.*
The Rev. JOHN SAMUEL BARON, *Brill.*
JOHN BROWN, Esq., *Kingston.*
HENRY ALEXANDER BROWN, Esq., *Kingston Grove.*
The Rev. GEORGE CHETWODE, *Chilton.*
JOHN FANE, Esq., Wormsley, *Lewknor Uphill.*
JOHN WILLIAM FANE, Esq., *Shirburn Lodge.*
CHARLES JOHN BAILLIE HAMILTON, Esq., *Thame Park.*
JOSEPH WARNER HENLEY, Esq., *Waterperry.*
HUGH HAMERSLEY, Esq., *Haseley House.*
The Rev. JOHN KIPLING, *Chilton.*
CHARLES SPENCER RICKETTS, Esq., *Dorton.*
CHARLES ALEXANDER SHEPPARD, Esq., *Great Milton.*
JOHN STONE, Esq., *Long Crendon.*
EDWARD WEBB, Esq., *Adwell.*

PAROCHIAL GUARDIANS.

NORTH DISTRICT.

ALBURY ....Mr. William King.	SHABBINGTON ..Mr. James Crook.
BRILL ....Mr. Michael Bond. Mr. T. Cooper Smith.	TIDDINGTON ....Mr. John Woodbridge.
CHILTON ....Mr. Joseph Osborne.	THOMLEY ....Mr. Richard Walker.
DORTON ....Mr. William Fuller.	WATERPERRY....Mr. Ezra Stallworthy.
ICKFORD ....Mr. John Guy.	WATERSTOCK ......Mr. Thomas Parsons.
LONG CRENDON ..Rev. Thomas Hayton. Mr. Robert Dodwell.	WORMINGHALL ...Mr. Thomas Sheen.
OAKLEY ....Mr. James Hudson.	

THAME DISTRICT.

ASTON ROWANT....Mr. William Harding.	SYDENHAM ....Mr. Stephen Croton.
CROWELL	TETSWORTH ......Mr. John Slatter.
EMMINGTON ......Mr. Robert Juggins.	THAME ....Charles Stone, Esq. Rev. Frederick Lee.
KINGSEY ....Mr. George North.	Mr. Stephen Whichello.

SOUTH DISTRICT.

ADWELL............	LEWKNOR ....Mr. George Carter.
ASCOTT .... .Mr. Edward Franklin.	LEWKNOR UPHILL Mr. Jesse Clift.
CHILWORTH ......Mr. Richard Crundall.	SHIRBURN..........Mr. John Green.
CHARLGROVE......Mr. Richard Stone.	SOUTH WESTON ....Mr. John Filbee.
EASINGTON ....Mr. John Puzey.	STOKE TALMAGE..Mr. John Sparks.
GREAT HASELEY .. Mr. Anthony Coghill.	WARPSGROVE......Mr. James Edwards.
GREAT MILTON ....Mr. Thomas Tomkins.	WHEATFIELD ......Rev. Edward Fanshawe Glanville.
LITTLE MILTON....Mr. James Fruin.	

OFFICERS OF THE UNION.

Clerk.
Mr. John Hollier, Thame.

Auditor.
Mr. Richard Bignell, Thame.

Treasurer.
Mr. Thomas Stone, Thame.

Medical Officers.
North District, Messrs. Lupton and Reynolds, Thame.
Thame District, Messrs. Lupton and Reynolds.
South District, Mr J W. Kimpton, Stadhampton.
Mr. Jesse Dutton, Stokenchurch.

Relieving Officers.
North District, Samuel Caporn, Long Crendon.
Thame District, Eden White, Thame.
South District, Vincent Fletcher, Little Milton

OFFICERS OF THE WORKHOUSE.

Chaplain.
The Rev. Amos Hayton.

Medical Officer.
Messrs. Lupton and Reynolds.

Master.
Mr. Henry Laman.

Matron.
Mrs. Laman.

Schoolmaster.
William Jaques.

Schoolmistress.
Harriet Lester.

Porter.
George Thomas Pulker.

ABOVE: The Station Wagon outside the Spread Eagle Hotel. The inn
sign was moved in the 1930s. BELOW: High Street in the age of the early
motor car.

On New Lines

The isolation and insularity of most English communities before the 19th century were due largely to the poor state of communications, especially the roads. A motley collection of dirt tracks and mud ways comprised the English Road System; repair was spasmodic (generally in the hands of parochial officials) and often ineffective. Piles of faggots or boulders were strewn over the worst chasms, but travel, even on horseback, was a dangerous occupation. Brown and Guest report an anecdote of a carter who drowned in a puddle on the Haddenham road. Lord Torrington punned that the road to Notley 'would tame the fiercest horse', and if the weary traveller managed to survive the jolting and jarring of the road surface, he could always become prey to highwaymen, such as the ones who robbed Lady Wenman in 1761 actually outside her stately home.

Some improvements had occurred by the 18th century, however, in consequence of the Turnpike Trusts set up by Act of Parliament. The Trusts maintained stretches in road by charging tolls to users and the toll-collecting was farmed out to bidders at an annual meeting at the Greyhound Inn. Some local turnpikes paid dividends to shareholders.

These new roads made travelling by coach a less daunting possibility, and it is known that by 1773 Thame had a weekly coach link direct to London. There were also coaches from Oxford to London, which could be joined at Tetsworth. Some of these journeys were two day affairs, but by 1834 a time of 4 or 5 hours was more usual. Thus the main alignment of roads in Thame up to the 19th century was to connect with the London Road, via Rycote Lane and the Postcombe Turnpike Road, rather than with Oxford, as nowadays. The stage coaches brought a certain amount of wealth, and some of Thame's prosperous inns date from this era, though the grandest, the Spread Eagle, was apparently built as a private house.

However, the improvements in turnpike roads had come too late to revive totally the flagging highway system, for new methods of conveyance were afoot. Although Thame was nowhere near any of the centres of the Industrial Revolution, it was to feel the impact of new modes of transport fairly early. The Oxford Canal was completed in 1790, and the Grand Junction reached Aylesbury in 1814. There was an impact on prices for bulk goods, such as coal, but the cost of road transport for the 13 mile journey to Oxford was almost as high as the Canal charge from the Leicester coalfield. Apparently, the cost of fuel (as much as 20s a ton in Thame) reduced some residents to burning cow clots and bean stubble. Telford, the engineer, did actually plan a canal from Abingdon to Aylesbury, passing near Thame, but the project was never realised.

But the 'canal revolution' was almost stillborn, for before it could make its full impact, it found itself under attack from another rival born of the Industrial Revolution—the steam railway. At the height of 'railway mania', schemes for lines were almost as prolific as road improvement plans are nowadays. The first proposed railway to Thame was Stephenson's projected line of 1845 from Aylesbury, which would have entered Thame behind the Prebendal, with a station just to the west of Cuttlebrook. Two other schemes were mooted that same year, both linking Thame with Oxford, and pursuing courses roughly similar to the remains of the present line. Eventually, Thame was linked to Princes Risborough in 1862. Before then, the London and North Western Railway had been luring potential rail passengers with a daily coach to Tring.

The first sod of the new line was cut at Towersey on 5 September 1859. However, the subscription list for the £140,000 capital required seems to have been slow in getting off the ground, and by February 1862 the *Thame Gazette* felt moved to deplore the slow progress being made in constructing the broad-gauge line. The line was completed in August 1862 (not without loss of life) and had an immediate impact on the town.

> 'Oh! Thame, thou hast triumphed, thy cause being just,
> With Victory's need on thy brow.
> Neither Wycombe or Aylesbury (Old Lady), I trust,
> Will slander or banter thee now'.

wrote a local poet. He had good reason to feel buoyant; Thame had 4 trains daily to London (one only on Sundays), for a return fare of 16s (1st Class) or 11s 6d (2nd Class). Henceforth, coal arrived at Thame by rail, and the local coaching services gradually diminished, and the turnpikes withered away; the Risborough one, for example, was discontinued on 1 January 1871.

The impact of the railway cannot be over-estimated. Although Thame did not expand physically very much as a result of its arrival, there were noticeable effects. Agricultural produce could be carried fresh to London; milk production, for example, expanded considerably. Coal became cheaper. Thame market attracted clientèle from a wider area. Trips and excursions to the London shows became regular events; a 'day trip' to Boulogne was even organised in 1877, though one wonders what sort of state the passengers were in after a 4.00 am start and a return at 5.30 am the next day! Perhaps they were cheered by the Brass Band, who accompanied them as far as Folkestone.

From the start, Thame had hoped that it would be the 'resting place, not the terminus', for the Railway, and the extension to Oxford was duly completed in May 1864. One of the contractors' locomotives for this work, being removed by road, sank in the dirt outside the Falcon Inn; 22 horses and several hours labour were needed to rescue it from its predicament. In April 1874, at a cost of £12,000, the line was relaid as Standard Guage.

The line was not without incident during its lifetime; several accidents to staff and passengers occurred, including an engine smashing into the engine shed at Thame in May 1864, and in 1874 the *Thame Gazette* noted 'a singular occurrence' when two trains on the single line track converged on each other near Thame; fortunately, they managed to stop in time.

Complaints about the service were almost simultaneous with its opening. The 'exorbitant fares' led some passengers to travel to Aylesbury by 'bus, and thence to London by train (costing 1s 5d less than going direct from Thame). Timetable alterations were quite frequent, and the service never really recovered from the serious curtailments during the 2nd World War. Although used as a diversion route for main-line trains on some occasions, the 'branch line' was finally closed in 1963, the track beyond Thame in the Oxford direction being lifted.

There were many other plans to bring railways to Thame, some being optimistic in the extreme, like the proposal in 1868 to link the town with Crendon, Chilton and Brill (for a mere £35,000).

But during the century of railway domination, roads too made a comeback. (Indeed, because stations acted as the centres for rural areas, railways sometimes actually stimulated road improvements.) In 1865, control over the repair of local roads passed to the Bullingdon Highway District; a local waywarden assumed responsibility for each parish. By 1876, adventurous velocipedists could hold bicycle races along the road to Aylesbury. The first motor 'bus to try its luck between the two towns ran in 1906, regular services to Oxford commencing in 1922. Such 'public transport' has of course declined relatively in recent years, as the private car and lorry jostle each other for possession of the highway.

ABOVE: The Ford at Thame, on the Oxford Road. The photograph shows the buildings which preceded West's Garage.

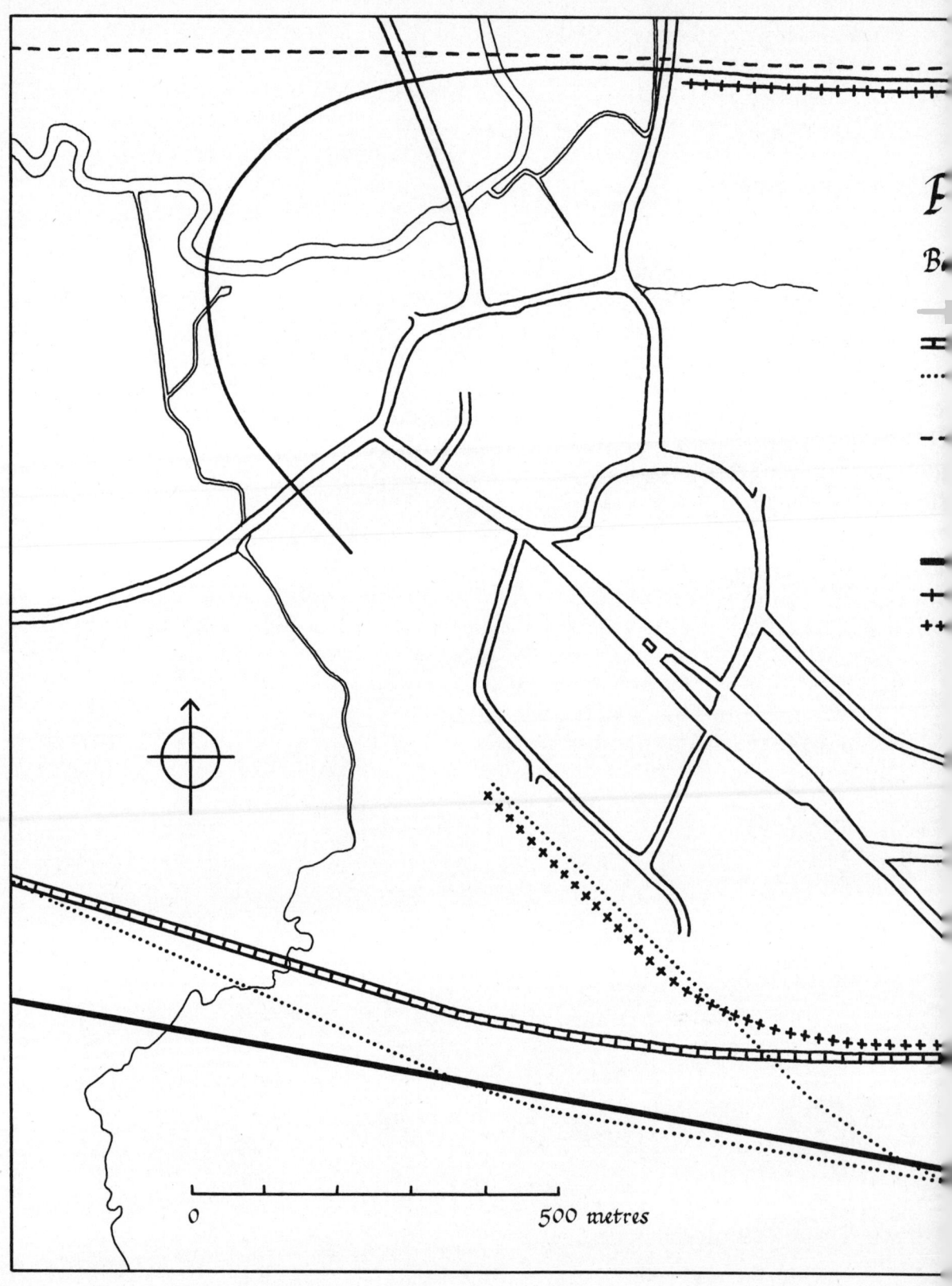

0   500 metres

Railways to Thame

in the County Record Office

and Aylesbury, 1845
Thame and High Wycombe, 1845
Witney, Cheltenham, Gloucester
endent Extension Railway, 1845
R., Tring to Oxford, 1852/3
don, Bucks. and West Midland
tion Railway, 1861
n, Bucks. and East Gloucs. Rly., 1865
be and Oxford Railway, 1854
and Aylesbury Railway, 1858/9
ry and Thame Railway, 1861

Projected railways in the Thame area.

Station

ABOVE: The Oxford Road, in more leisured days. The ford is on the right.
BELOW: Troops embark at the station during the First World War.

TIME TABLE for the month of Sept. of the **GREAT WESTERN RAILWAY** (Thame Aylesbury and Wycombe Branches), and of the **GREAT CENTRAL RAILWAY** (Haddenham Branch).

DOWN TRAINS.	WEEK DAYS.																			SUNDAYS.			
	A.M	A.M	A.M	A.M	A.M	A.M	A.M	P.M	P.M		P.M	P.M	P.M	P.M	P.M	P.M	P.M	P.M	P.M	A.M	A.M	P.M	P.M
PADDINGT'N dep.	...	7 0	...	8 10	...	9 32	...	1147	1 25	...	2 35	4 3	...	5 20	...	6 20	7 20	9 0		...	9 23	...	9 0
Maidenhead dep																							
Wycombe { arr.	...	7 53	...	9 7	9 43	1022	1222	1232	2 14	...	3 25	4 52	5 37	6	6 6	24	7	6 8	8 9	58	9 47	1020	7 27	9 53
{ dep	7 55	...	9 11	9 45	1039	1224	1236	2 16	...	3 28	4 55	5 39	6	8 6	26	7	8 8	10 10	0	9 50	1022	7 30	9 59
W. Wycombe ,,	8 0	...	9 16	9 50	1044	1229	1241	2 21	...	3 33	5	0 5	44	6 13	6 31	7	13 8	15 10	5	9 55	1027	7 35	10 2
Saunderton ,,	...	...	9 22	9 55	1049	1234	1246	2 26	...	3 38	5	5 5	49	6 18	6 36	7	18 8	21 10	10	10 0	1032	7 40	10 8
Risboro' .... arr.	8 10	...	9 28	10 1	1055	1240	1252	2 32	...	3 44	5 11	5 54	6 24	6 42	7 24	8 27	1016			10 6	1038	7 46	1014
Risboro' dep.	...	...	9 37	...	1056	...	1258	2 33	...	3 59	5 13	...	6 26	...	7 30	8 28	1017			...	1043	...	1017
Lt. Kimble ,,	...	...	9 43	...	11 2	...	1 6	2 39	...	3 56	5 19	...	6 32	...	7 38	8 34	1023			...	...	...	
AYLESB'Y arr.	...	...	9 52	...	1110	...	1 15	2 47	...	4 5	5 27	...	6 40	...	7 45	8 42	1030			...	1055	...	1030
Risboro' ... dep.	...	8 11	9 31	...	1110		1255	...	...	3 48	...	...	...	...	7 27		P.M.			...	1041	...	1016
Bledlow ... ,,	...	8 17	9 36	...	1115		1 1	...	...	3 53	...	...	...	...	7 32					...	1046	...	1022
THAME ... ,,	...	8 24	9 46	...	1122	Tues. only.	1 12	...	...	4 5	...	...	...	...	7 43	9 40				...	1059	...	1031
Tiddington ,,	...	8 33	9 57	...			1 21	...	...	4 18	...	...	...	...	7 52	9 49				...	1112	...	1040
Wheatley... ,,	...	8 43	10 6	...	...		1 29	...	...	4 28	...	...	...	...	8 0	9 57				...	1122	...	1050
Littlemore ,,	...	8 52	1016	...	...		1 40	...	...	4 38	...	...	...	...	8 9	10 6				...	1130	...	11 0
OXFORD ...... arr.	...	9 0	1025	...	...		1 47	...	...	4 45	...	...	...	...	8 15	1015				...	1138	...	11 7
Risboro' ... deP.	7 26	...	...	9 54	...	1 15	...	...	...	...	...	...	6 46	...	...			10 8		...	7 48	...	
Haddenham ,,	7 35	...	...	10 3	...	1 24	...	...	...	...	...	...	6 57	...				1019		...	7 59	...	
Wotton ... ,,	7 44	...	...	1012	...	1 33	...	...	...	...	...	...	7 9	...	SATS. ONLY.			1030		...	8 10	...	
Akeman St. ,,	7 49	...	...	1017	...	1 38	...	...	...	...	...	...	7 16	...				1035		...	8 15	...	
Calvert ... arr.	7 58	...	...	1026	...	1 46	...	...	...	...	...	...	7 26	...				1047		...	8 25	...	

UP TRAINS.	WEEK DAYS																		SUNDAYS.			
	A.M	A.M	A.M	A.M	A.M	A.M	A.M	A.M	P.M	P.M	P.M	P.M	P.M	P.M	P.M	P.M	P'M	A.M	A.M	P.M	P.M
Calvert...... dep.	...	...	8 31	...	...	...	9 57	...	1239	...	...	...	5 0	5 54	...	...		...	8 40	...	6 56
Akeman St. ,,	...	...	8 40	...	...	...	10 6	...	1248	...	...	...	5 0	6 3	...	...		...	8 50	...	7 5
Wotton...... ,,	...	...	8 45	...	...	...	1011	...	1253	...	...	...	5 5	6 8	...	...		...	8 55	...	7 10
Haddenham ,,	...	...	8 54	...	...	...	1020	...	1 2	...	...	...	5 14	7 17	...	...		...	9 5	...	7 19
Risboro' ,,	...	...	9 4	...	...	...	1030	...	1 12	...	...	...	5 23	7 27	...	...		...	9 15	...	7 29
OXFORD ...... dep.	...	7 45	...	...	8 25	...	1120	...	2 28	...	...		6 20	8 50	6 40	...	5 55	...			
Littlemore ,,	...	7 56	...	...	8 34	...	1129	...	2 40	...	...		6 30	9 0	6 50	...	6 5	...			
Wheatley ... ,,	...	8 7	...	...	8 44	...	1139	...	2 50	...	Tues. only.		6 42	9 10	7 3	...	6 16	...			
Tiddington ,,	...	8 19	...	...	8 53	...	1146	...	2 57	...			6 54	9 18	7 17	...	6 24	...			
THAME ... ,,	...	8 31	...	...	9 6	...	1157	...	3 7	4 30	Sats. only.		7 6	9 28	7 35	...	6 34	...			
Bledlow ... ,,	...	8 41	...	...	9 17	...	12 7	...	3 16	4 40			7 17		7 45	...	6 44	...			
Risboro' ... arr.	...	8 47	...	...	9 22	...	1212	...	3 21	4 44			7 22		7 50	...	6 49	...			
AYLESB'Y dep.	...	...	7 50	...	9	1010	...	1150	...	2 0	5 4 50	...	5 50	...	7 5	7 30	...	6 32	...		
Lt. Kimble ,,	...	...	7 59	...	9 13	1018	...	12 2	...	2 8	3 13 4 58	...	5 58	...	7 13	7 40	...	6 42	...		
Risboro' arr.	...	...	8 5	...	9 19	1024	...	1210	...	2 14	3 19 5 6	...	6 4	...	7 19	7 46	...	6 48	...		
Risboro' dep.	...	8 51	8 7	...	9 28	1025	1034	1214	1 15	2 16	3 25 5 9	...	6 5	7 16	7 31	...	7 53	9 19	6 53	7 30
Saunderton ,,	...	8 59	8 14	...	9 35	1032	1041	1221	1 22	2 23	3 32 5 16	...	6 12	...	7 39	...	8 0	9 26	7 0	7 37
W. Wycombe ,,	...	9 4	8 19	...	9 40	1037	1046	1226	1 27	2 28	3 37 5 21	...	6 17	...	7 46	...	8 6	9 31	7 6	7 43
Wycombe { arr.	...	9 9	8 23	...	9 45	1042	1051	1231	1 32	2 33	3 42 5 25	...	6 22	7 27	7 51	...	8 11	9 36	7 11	7 49
{ dep	...	9 14	8 30	...	9 48	1044	1055	1234	1 35	2 35	3 44 5 35	...	6 24	...	7 55	...	8 14	9 39	7 15	7 50
Maidenhead arr.	...	...	...	...	...	...	...	...	...	...	...	...	...	...	...	...	...	...	...	...	
PADDING'N arr.	...	10 2	9 15	...	1035	1139	...	1 20	...	3 25	4 30 6 27	...	7 20	...	9 30	...	10 0	...	8 17	...	

Although every care is taken to ensure accuracy in this Table, we do not hold ourselves responsible for any error that may inadvertently occur.]

Railway time-table, 1907.

Thame railway station, by Henry Taunt.

ABOVE: A coaching scene in the High Street about 100 years ago.
BELOW: The original West's Garage, with car display outside.

The Dissenters

From 1660, Anglicanism was the established religion in England; adherents of other sects and beliefs were excluded from public office, and some actively persecuted. Yet paradoxically, the 18th century was a low ebb in England's established Church, and a high tide in Prostestant Nonconformity. Thame reflected, in microcosm, these national trends.

Thame had but 6 vicars between 1629 and 1795. During their period of office, the Church acquired a large number of substantial tablets to the worthier (or wealthier?) inhabitants. Yet beneath this external placidity lay an undercurrent of deep controversy and even hatred. There was resentment at having to pay tithe and church rates for the upkeep of the clergy and the fabric. In 1713, William Loosley was presented (brought before the authorities of the Peculiar) for refusing to pay his rate and suggesting it would be cheaper to pull the church down and re-erect it. In fairness, he was probably incensed by the fact that the church rate was being levied annually, whereas in theory it ought only to have been collected when necessity arose. Apart from the fabric, the money went towards the Easter Monday feast and the salaries of officials like the organist and the dog-whipper (who received £1 per annum).

The Church continued to exercise discipline and moral authority over its parishioners. John Thomlinson and the wife of George Ellis were admonished in 1608 for being 'lockt into a rome (room) together very suspiciously by her husband's report'. The father of an illegitimate child had publicly to 'purge' himself in the Parish Church in 1675. Most extraordinary of all, Thomas Heath was summoned in 1696 'for cohabiting in an unlawful manner with the wife of George Fuller of Chinnor, for the space of 3 weeks about 3 months since haveing bought her of her husband at 2d the pound . . .'

Less momentous, perhaps, were the presentations for non-attendance. In 1670, 90 people were accused of this offence and subsequent non-payment of dues to the vicar. Yet the clergy themselves were not blameless, for several 17th and 18th century vicars of Thame held the living in plurality with other local parishes.

Although some people were inclined to see 'Papists' at the bottom of every threat to the established order, there is little evidence of the 'old religion' in the Thame area before the present century. Certain members of the Wenman family at Thame

Park, and the Clerk family of North Weston were recusants in the early years of the 17th century, and from 1766 until 1800, a Roman Catholic priest performed rites at Thame Park for Lady Eleanor Bertie. But apart from these, and the group of 50 exiled French clergy during the Napoleonic period, there is little evidence of activity. The present Catholic Church was erected in 1922, and its recent extension testifies to the growth of the community in recent years.

Puritanism, or Presbyterianism, grew up within the fabric of the Anglican Church, but disconnected itself from the parent body during the Civil War. A census of 1676 recorded a total of 100 'utter dissenters' in Thame, but a meeting of 200 Presbyterians and Anabaptists in a private house had occurred 7 years earlier. The house of Edward Howes was first licensed as a meeting place for this group in 1672, served by an ejected ex-Anglican called John Nott. The successors to this group acquired a site in Sun Yard and erected a Chapel. The Minister of this, Mathew Leeson, also ran a school which the notorious radical John Wilkes attended as a pupil. However, Presbyterianism had fizzled out in Thame by the turn of the 19th century, and the Methodist congregation had acquired the Sun Yard Chapel.

The Independents, or Congregationalists, had also got bricks and mortar together by this time, when a group belonging to the Countess of Huntingdon's Connexion converted a pub into a chapel. A new congregation was formed in 1821, and moved to a new chapel in 1827 (now the Masonic Hall). By 1851, it could return congregations of over 100 on Sunday morning and 166 for the evening, together with attendant Sunday Schools. A doctrinal rift occurred in 1860, but by 1871 matters had recovered sufficiently for a new chapel to be erected (the present building in Upper High Street).

Methodism sprang up in Thame following two visits by Wesley to the town in 1778 and 1782. On the first occasion, the wind and the threat of a troublesome mob drove him inside the former Presbyterian Chapel. Inspired by his speech and the healing of a bed-ridden patient, Methodism grew apace in the town. After a series of converted buildings, the movement erected a new chapel in Upper High Street in 1853; despite the setback of a serious fire in 1875, the movement flourished.

Two groups of Primitive Methodists also flourished—one based in Moreton, which had an attendance of 50 in the 1851 census, and the other in Thame which eventually came to rest in East Street. The groups later merged back into mainstream Methodism. 20th century ecumenicalism (and economy) has resulted in a link up with the Congregationalists, and the Methodist Church now houses a photographer's studio.

A group of 32 Quakers existed in 1676; but the movement's most active member was the 19th century grocer William Wheeler who sustained a group in a building in his garden in East Street.

The Salvation Army fared less well. Herbert Booth, son of the great General, visited Thame in 1887, but he was hooted and booed and rubbish was thrown at him. A second visit apparently resulted in a tricycle battle outside the Town Hall!

The Baptists were certainly established in Thame by 1690, but probably had no chapel here until 1825, when a building in Rooks Lane was in use. The movement had divided by mid-century, with Thomas Juggins leading a splinter group in a meeting room in Friday Street. By 1854 unity was restored and worship held in the Sun Yard Chapel, now in its third (and final) Nonconformist phase. A new chapel followed in 1865 (in Park Street—the present building) and the movement, having survived certain vicissitudes early in this century, was able to purchase the old Primitive Methodist Chapel in East Street as a Church Hall in 1957.

Nonconformity tended to diminish its impact on the established church by its tendency to fragment; but undoubtedly the movement had a fair influence on the shaping of Thame. The groups were capable of sinking their differences when the occasion demanded, sharing chapels, choirs and schools, and lending weight to the Temperance Movement. They were equally capable of rivalling the Anglican Church, championing the Thame British School against its National rival. There were accusations of discrimination on both sides; a separate system of shops existed in the town for church and chapel. Numerically, Chapel ran Church very close; in terms of Sunday School numbers, the Nonconformists were actually ahead. The writing was already printed large upon the wall by the time of the 1851 religious census which gave statistical backing to what many had known for a long time.

How did the Anglican Church respond to this challenge? The Church was certainly extensively refurbished, being restored and repaired in 1843-5 and 1889. During this latter restoration, all galleries were removed and certain alterations done to roof and windows. The furnishings and tombs had already been subjected to a game of ecclesiastical musical chairs, including moving the Quatremains tombs. But even in its revamped guise, the Church could not conceal the fact that it was losing authority. The scope and powers of the Churchwardens for example were eroded by the arrival of new supra-parochial authorities such as the Poor Law Guardians. Dissent began seriously to challenge the Church's educational and religious pre-eminence.

In such a situation, leadership was needed. The Rev T. T. Lee (1795-1841) struggled hard; he claimed 35 years in the parish without a month's leave, and congregations of 600 were achieved by mid-century. By contrast, the Rev J. Prosser (1841-1872) found popular acclaim for his charitable nature and kindliness towards children, but success in filling the church eluded him. There was criticism of his 'Calvinist' beliefs; carping about the expense of £2,000 on a new, large vicarage; and in his last years attempts were made 'to secure an effective ministry' in the town. He resigned at the age of 80. Things appeared rather to have gone to seed by then. A flock of 300 sheep grazed in the churchyard; a fanciful letter in the *Thame Gazette* of April 1867 deplored the 'disgusting possibility of eating mutton fattened at the graves of our fathers'. In the churchyard extension, 6 hogs were found to be grubbing in 1857. The sexton had to be reprimanded for drunkenness in 1865. The vicar astonished his congregation on one occasion by leapfrogging the sanctuary rails, and, the ultimate of 'shameful events', turned up to preach a sermon in his night-shirt.

Subsequent events were brighter; the choir and several classes flourished, a mission church was built in 1884, and a hall begun in 1913. By then, however, the heat of rivalry was passing, and all churches began to look to safeguarding their own congregations in an age of increasing apathy. Amalgamations and ecumenism have replaced the old rivalries.

The Church in 1889.

ABOVE: The original vicarage, demolished in 1841. BELOW: The
present vicarage.

ABOVE: The Church, as photographed by Henry Taunt, showing the
'barbarous tracery' of the East window, removed during the restoration of
last century. BELOW: A view towards the Church across Church Meadow,
taken about the turn of the century.

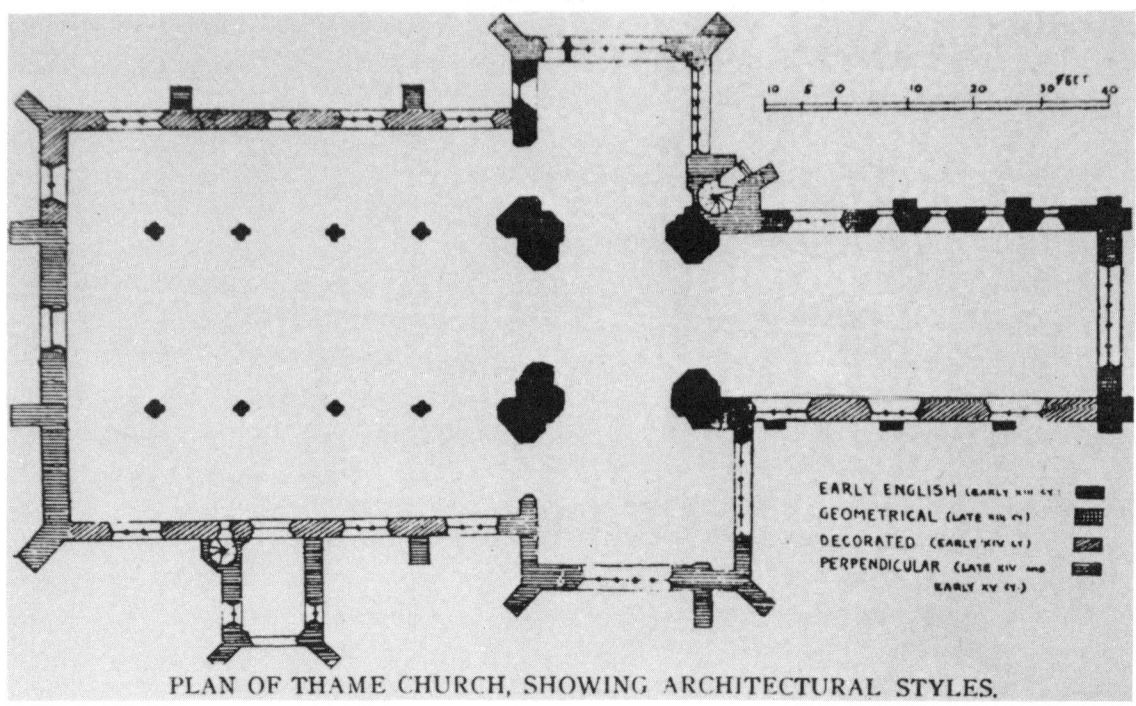

PLAN OF THAME CHURCH, SHOWING ARCHITECTURAL STYLES.

EARLY ENGLISH (EARLY XIII CT.)
GEOMETRICAL (LATE XIII CT.)
DECORATED (EARLY XIV CT.)
PERPENDICULAR (LATE XIV AND
EARLY XV CT.)

ABOVE: The Church, from a print of 1868. (BL) BELOW: Plan of the
Church.

115

ABOVE: Inside arrangements of the Church, drawn before restoration and removals. BELOW LEFT: The ancient chalice of the Church. RIGHT: The first building of St Joseph's Roman Catholic Church.

A RETURN

~~ticulars~~ to be inquired into respecting the undermentioned CHURCH or CHAPEL in England,
belonging to the United Church of England and Ireland.

~~mutatis mutandis~~,) will be obtained with respect to Churches belonging to the Established Church in
~~the~~ Episcopal Church there, and also from Roman Catholic Priests, and from the Ministers of every other
~~Religious~~ Denomination throughout Great Britain, with respect to their Places of Worship.]

NAME and DESCRIPTION of CHURCH or CHAPEL.

Saint Mary's

~~WHERE~~ SITUATED.	Parish, Ecclesiastical Division or District, Township or Place	Superintendent Registrar's District	County and Diocese
	Thame	*John Hollier*	*Oxford*

~~WHEN~~ CONSECRATED ~~OR~~ LICENSED	Under what Circumstances CONSECRATED or LICENSED	*N*
Consecrated	*Before 1800.*	

~~In~~ the case of a CHURCH or CHAPEL CONSECRATED or LICENSED since the 1st January, 1800; state

HOW OR BY WHOM ERECTED	COST, how Defrayed
	By Parliamentary Grant ....
	Parochial Rate ....
	„ Private Benefaction, or Subscription, or from other Sources...... }
	Total Cost......£

V.		VI.	
HOW ENDOWED		**SPACE AVAILABLE FOR PUBLIC WORSHIP**	
.... *160* £	Pew Rents........... £ *none*	Free Sittings *400*
.... *21*	Fees .... *{23.12.0*	Other Sittings *590*
	Dues	
~~Amount En~~ }	Easter Offerings ..... *none*	
	Other Sources .... *none*	Total Sittings... *990*

~~Estimated~~ Number of Persons attending **Divine Service** on Sunday, March 30, 1851.			AVERAGE NUMBER OF ATTENDANTS during Months next preceeding March 30, 1851. (See Instruction VII.)		
	Morning	Afternoon	Evening		Morning	Afternoon	Evening

	Morning	Afternoon	Evening		Morning	Afternoon	Evening
~~General~~ Congregation }	*510*	*did not attend as a school*	*404*	General Congregation Sunday Scholars }	*550*	✗	*500*
~~Sunday~~ Scholars	*140*				*140*		
Total..	*650*		*404*	Total...	*690*		*500*

~~RE~~MARKS *I have much pleasure in giving you the above information; as I shall have in replying to any further inquiries.*

I certify the foregoing to be a true and correct Return to the best of my belief.

~~Witness~~ my hand this *31st* day of *March* 1851.

IX. (Signature) ___*James Prosser*___

(Official Character) *Vicar of Thame* of the above named

(Address by Post) *Vicarage, Thame, Oxon* *Parish of Thame, Oxon.*

Page from the 1851 religious census, showing the return for the Parish Church. Attendances were to decline dramatically in the later years of the Rev Prosser's incumbency. (PRO)

A RETURN
OF THE SEVERAL PARTICULARS TO BE INQUIRED INTO RESPECTING THE UNDERMENTIONED
PLACE OF PUBLIC RELIGIOUS WORSHIP.

[N.B.—A similar Return will be obtained from the Clergy of the Church of England, and also from the Ministers of every other Religious Denomination throughout Great Britain.]

I.	II.			III.	IV.	V.	VI.	VII.			VIII.			IX.
Name or Title of Place of Worship	Where Situate; specifying the			Religious Denomination	When Erected	Whether a Separate and Entire Building	Whether used exclusively as a Place of Worship (Except for a Sunday School)	Space available for Public Worship			Estimated Number of Persons attending Divine Service on Sunday, March 30, 1851			REMARKS
	Parish or Place	District	County					Number of Sittings already Provided		Free Space or Standing Room for	Morning	Afternoon	Evening	
	(1)	(2)	(3)					Free Sittings (4)	Other Sittings (5)					
Baptist Chapel	Parish of Thame	Thame District	Oxford	Particular Baptist	1825	Yes	Yes	All	None	Only the aisle not intended for the ordinary room	General Congregation 37 / Sunday Scholars 45	103 / 47	34 / —	This return is the average number for the last twelve months. The twenty copies which were given in number from witheld.
											Total.. 82	150	34	
											Average Number of Attendants during months (See Instruction VIII.) General Congregation / Sunday Scholars / Total..			

I certify the foregoing to be a true and correct Return to the best of my belief. Witness my hand this 31st day of March 1851.

x (Signature) ...... Stephen Walker

(Official Character) Minister of the above-named Place of Worship.

(Address by Post) High Street Thame Oxon

The return for the Baptist Chapel.

156-7 10-19

118

ABOVE: Auctioneer's building, once a chapel. (QPS) BELOW: Upper High Street, showing the Methodist and Congregationalist Chapels. They are now combined as the United Reformed Church in the far building.

119

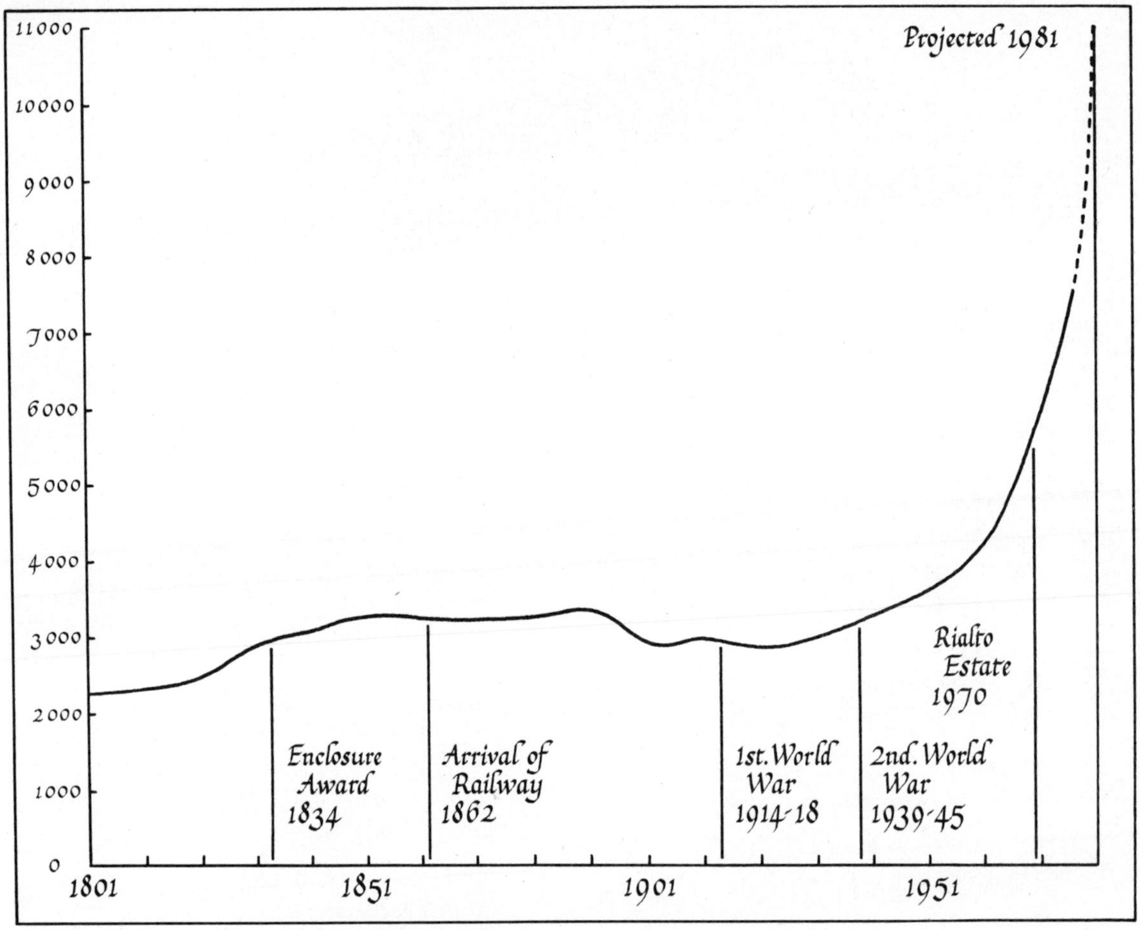

Population Graph

- 11 000
- 10 000
- 9 000
- 8 000
- 7 000
- 6 000
- 5 000
- 4 000
- 3 000
- 2 000
- 1 000
- 0

Projected 1981

Enclosure
Award
1834

Arrival of
Railway
1862

1st. World
War
1914-18

2nd. World
War
1939-45

Rialto
Estate
1970

1801   1851   1901   1951

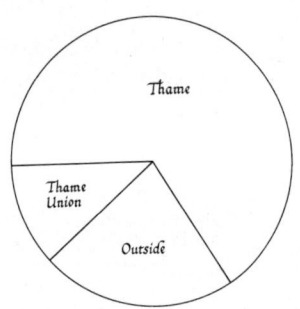

Thame

Thame
Union

Outside

Population graph of Thame. The 'sag' in the middle of the last century is common to several rural areas.

LEFT: A chart to show mobility in Thame in 1851.

Of Life and Leisure

Who were the people of Thame in the last century? What work did they do? What was the social structure of the community? Was Thame a stable, or a fluctuating community? Some of these questions can be answered by reference to directories and the census returns.

The most straightforward task is to compute the population trends of the town. The stagnation during the middle of the 19th century is most notable. Following that, it is possible to compile a mobility index to show the extent of movement around the country as revealed by the census, such as that for 1851, before the railway had arrived. As expected, a large proportion of the population was locally bred; however, there were a fair number of migrants, some from quite exotic locations, such as France, Ireland, and even the East Indies.

Family size is not easy to work out from the census returns. If we exclude young married couples under the age of thirty (on the grounds that many of them were just beginning families) and older married couples over the age of 50 (because their families had often left home), we are left with the following distribution for 1851:

Number of children	Total of families
1	29
2	48
3	49
4	40
5	42
6	27
7	12
8	3
9	1
10	1

The figures still seem to include a lot of younger couples, so one would have to conclude that average family size was about 3 to 5 children in Thame at this time. However, there are also substantial differences between different areas; Old Thame, for example, has a significantly higher average family size than New Thame.

So much for demographic considerations; the stagnation of Thame's population figures in the 19th century points to the relative lack of development in the town. Traditional skills and jobs persisted for a long time, 'industry' being on a small scale. A sizeable proportion of the local population has always been engaged in agriculture or ancillary occupations, but there has always been a goodly number involved in craft or commercial occupations.

Information on employment is very sketchy before the 19th century. Due to a shortage of change, some Thame traders in the 17th century issued Trade Tokens, from which it appears, for example, that two hatters, two mercers, two chandlers, a tailor and a draper existed in Thame. Undoubtedly this only represents the tip of the iceberg. Clockmakers are known to have plied their craft in Thame from the mid-18th century–the Spread Eagle was originally a clockmaker's residence.Evidence of the activities of the professional classes in Thame can perhaps be judged by the wordy monumental inscriptions in the Church. Surgeons and solicitors seem unusually prolific in the area, and 18th century monuments also exist in Thame Church to a mason, a bodice maker, an apothecary, a carpenter, and an ironmonger—to cite but a few, and these must have been men of some substance to merit commemoration. Many of the memorial plaques simply list the deceased's occupation as 'gent', which could cover a multitude of sins. Thomas Crews (died 1731), for example, was a noted philanthropist and according to Lee, his monumental inscription originally contained these lines:

'In the morning when sober, in the evening when mellow,
You scarce ever met such a jolly good fellow.'

Bishop Wilberforce, obviously lacking a sense of humour, had the offending couplet removed.

Our information is more systematic when we reach the 19th century, for the census returns supply details of occupations, and commercial directories exist which list the tradesmen in the town. From these sources it might well appear possible to attempt some sort of occupational index. However, the process is fraught with innumerable difficulties. The directories list only tradesmen and professional people, and cannot be relied upon to be exhaustive in their coverage. The census is even more of a snare for the unwary. A literal head-count would result in 'scholars' and 'housewives' as the largest categories. However, one suspects that many wives with husbands in craft, trade or agricultural occupations took a large share in their husbands' work. In some cases, the census enumerators took this into account, and wives are occasionally designated 'farmer's wife' or 'innkeeper's wife'. Elsewhere, wives sometimes pursued quite different jobs; a favoured combination in the Thame area for the wives of agricultural labourers seems to have been to take on lacemaking. The situation becomes even more complex when children are taken into account. There are sometimes families listed in the census with 'children' well into their 20s, with no specific occupation listed, so one simply has to guess how they earned their keep. Lastly, any system of classification is subject to error, as many of the terms used for the different occupations are only loose descriptions, and all one can hope to do is indicate the broad areas of employment, rather than produce any grandiose generalisations about social class. Even then, some entries in the 1851 census defy categorisation. Innkeepers commonly seem to pursue two jobs: during the daytime they were apparently bricklayers, glaziers or builders.

Some trades and crafts flourished especially over the years. A wool-stapling business has been in Thame since 1750. Fell-mongering and tanning were other thriving lines of business, whilst the reedy banks of the river Thame supplied the basket and chair-making crafts. Brick-making and brewing had an intermittent existence in the town. The poor quality of Thame's water was responsible for the demise of the latter trade, but the town's tipplers had no real cause for concern as the town continued until the early 20th century to be excessively well-endowed with ale-houses and inns. Of the pubs that survived over the years, some underwent a period of metamorphosis. The Spread Eagle gained in importance after the closure of the Red Lion and Greyhound inns during the 19th century. It was never a coaching inn, but had extensive stabling. A certain off-beat notoriety itself attached to the place during the ownership of John Fothergill in the 1930s. Whether the curious assortment of guests or the rude eccentricities of the landlord provided the greater interest is open to debate. Fothergill disliked Thame and its people, and one can guess that the feeling was reciprocated. However, his splendid ironwork sign still stands.

Yet Thame's attractions were not confined to the static occupation of drinking. Sports of various kinds flourished. Cock-fighting survived to the 20th century; bull-baiting almost certainly existed the century before, taking place in the old Hog Fair (opposite the present Catholic Church). But Thame has a greater claim to fame in the ring than mere animals, for one of the most famous of early prize-fighters, James Figg, was a native of the town. He was 'a man of remarkable athletic strength and agility, and signalized himself greatly over any of his country competitors, in the art of cudgel-playing, single-stick and other gymnastic exercises'. He became a popular performer:

'From Figg's theatre, he will not miss a night
Though cocks and bulls, and Irish women, fight.'

wrote a contemporary about an ardent spectator. Figg died in 1734. 'I will fight any man in England' he had boasted, and indeed, he is reputed to have lost only one fight in the whole of his career.

Hunting was popular in the area during the last century. The Earl of Abingdon seems to have kept the first local pack of hounds, at Rycote during the 1770s, and the South Oxfordshire Hunt evolved some 70 years later. The hare and fox were the main quarry, but a stag hunt was organised in 1856 under Baron Rothschild, when the beast was killed at Priestend. The *Thame Gazette* regularly featured hearty hunting tales in the last century, including one about a crafty fox who eluded the hunt by escaping down a chimney in 1859! Pigeon, sparrow and rook shooting also took place quite regularly and steeple-chasing between Thame and Tetsworth seems to have been regular at the time.

Less energetically, cricket was played in the town by 1770, probably on the Hog

Fair. The club, 'defunct for many years' was revived in 1862, and played on a variety of meadows. The recreation ground was opened by subscription in 1872, when a match was staged between 22 players on one side, and 11 on the other. The present town club possibly enjoys its most picturesque venue nowadays, with the Church as a backcloth.

Soccer began in town in 1883, when a club was formed, and matches played on the recreation ground. Soccer was for many years the premier game at both the Grammar and County schools, and the local team enjoyed some success in county competitions. The present popularity of the sport has brought about an expansion in teams and facilities.

Angling and shooting appear to have been popular during the last century, and rugby flourished after the Grammar School adopted it as its major sport in the 1920s. More recent times have brought about a swing to indoor and individual sports, such as tennis, squash, bowls, badminton and judo, and Thame has slowly acquired the facilities for these.

But for many people, the major entertainment during the year must have been the travelling shows and fairs which arrived regularly in Thame throughout the year. The Michaelmas Hiring Fair took place in October, and even in the mid-19th century, shepherds and dairymaids could be obtained in this way. Circuses regularly visited the town, bringing a wide range of exotic beasts and feats of equestrian skill. The children of the Workhouse were entertained free by Wombwell's Menagerie in 1866, and many companies paraded in the town before the show began. Even nowadays, Thame is still brought to a halt by the giant amusement fair which fills out the entire High Street for three days in late September. Thame Show, now the biggest one-day event in the county, coincides with the September fair. It began life relatively humbly as the shop window for the Thame Agricultural Society in 1855. The competitive classes included ploughing, shepherding, rick-building, thatching and hedging in the early days. At one stage, it was combined with the floral and vegetable displays of the Horticultural Society, but this ended in 1888.

Less transient entertainment was readily available in the town. The Thame Institute provided a wide range of talks, recitals and concerts of a morally improving nature. Founded in 1845, its members were treated to dissertations on topics as diverse as 'Our relations with China', 'Martin Luther', and 'Female education of the industrious classes'. There were 72 members in 1860, and five years later a total of 900 books existed in the library. In addition, a wide range of newspapers could be consulted between the hours of 9 am and 10 pm. A Reading Society also existed in 1857. The Institute, which occupied a substantial building in the High Street, amalgamated with Thame Fire Service Social Club in 1949.

Dr Foolkes of the Grammar School held concerts in the school hall in the 1860s (no difficulty, of course, since the Reverend Gentleman was doing his best to empty the school of pupils), and a choral society started in 1857. Despite many vicissitudes, the tradition of choral singing lives on in Thame to the present day. The most famous musical group in Thame, however, was the Brass Band, which started up about 1822, and which by dubious means later acquired the prefix 'royal'. The band was in attendance at all ceremonial occasions, and also gave concerts in neighbouring towns. Thame acquired a cinema in 1914, initially in Chinnor Road, and later in North Street. The Grand closed its doors in 1967, victim of high costs and bingo.

For those of a more sober disposition, there were the activities of the Temperance Society, which held an annual festival in April during the years of the last century. Its activities generated much vehement debate in the local press, but it must have felt its influence rather circumscribed by the bountiful supply of drinking places in the town. A temperance hotel is mentioned in the *Thame Gazette* of 14 August 1877, but further details are lacking.

On the whole, the major political events of the 18th and 19th centuries seem to have had little impact upon the everyday life of the town, whose existence was moulded more closely around economic factors such as the price of bread. However, national events occasionally had local repercussions. A meeting to demand the repeal of the Test Acts is recorded in 1732. More dramatic radicalism had to be faced 60 years later, when some 50 refugee French clergy fleeing from the Terror of Revolutionary France were accommodated by the Rev Lee. Moreover, in the years following 1805, some 120 French prisoners of war were billeted in the town, including 16 in the cellar of the Bird Cage Inn. They formed their own masonic lodge whilst in captivity, and were apparently let out on parole during the daytime. Five of them took advantage of this to abscond in 1806. Some, however, found Thame more congenial than Napoleonic France, and married locally.

Thame responded to the defence of King and Country by forming a troop of Yeoman Cavalry in 1798 and a later corps acted as a police force in the troubled times of the early years of the 19th century. A new Rifle Corps was established in 1860 as the Eighth Detachment of the Oxfordshire Volunteers (again, in response to a Napoleon), and tried to stir up the residual but dormant nationalism of the town by stirring verse:

> 'Ye men of Thame, ye are so Tame,
> Your town is almost lost to fame
> . . . let not the stigma last, I pray
> Enrol yourselves this very day.'

(the first of many heroic doggerels on their activities which appeared in the *Thame Gazette*). The Oxfordshire Yeomanry were the local 'professional' army troop, and held camps and parades in the town, including one in 1907 on Barley Hill Field attended by Winston Churchill. Troops were often billeted in the town *en route* to manouevres.

The event of war in 1914 brought home the realities of the situation. Some 587 men enlisted, whilst others less suited for the Front were drafted into the Volunteers for guard duties. The derelict old Boys' Grammar School was turned into a hospital, and some refugees from Belgium and (less exotically) the East End were billeted here. The depredations of war which had eroded public services and made food and supplies scarce were however soon forgotten in the junketings of Armistice Day, when a crowd of several thousands thronged the streets by the Town Hall. A war memorial was erected near the old Whitehound Pond, and opened by Lloyd George in 1921. The pond itself was subsumed by the Pearce Memorial of 1926, which must have been something of a blessing. The water in the old pond had been so stagnant that horses refused to drink from it, and it was a source of danger to animals and human beings alike; an unfortunate lady 'wandered' into there by mistake in January 1859. A gallant gentleman waded in to save her from a dreadful fate, but in her struggles she apparently went under several times.

The Second World War probably impinged more closely upon the inhabitants of the town, although the first casualty did not occur until April 1940. As before, evacuees arrived in force, and at the John Hampden School, pupils were taught in shifts. Air raid shelters were built at the school, and also in High Street and Upper High Street. A few bombs did actually fall in the area. The local inhabitants busied themselves in projects to raise money for weapons, tanks, Spitfires, and even a warship. VE Day was celebrated in style, with dancing and bonfires. As a War Memorial, the Elms was purchased for £8,000 and opened in 1948 as a public park and recreation area.

If we were to go back in time 100 years, the Thame of 1878 would strike us as being remarkably similar in basic shape, a shape that indeed had survived from the Middle Ages. Many more houses than now would have preserved their original fronts, but the pictures of local photographers such as Taunt and Payne display a remarkable continuity for most buildings with the present day. There was little Victorian sprawl or remodelling. The railway generated a small terraced suburb, and there are one or two stern examples of Victorian technicolour brickwork, but on the whole, facades remained unaltered. Of the public buildings of the last century, the Court House (slightly apologetically Romanesque in style) dates from 1861. The Town Hall was built in 1886, unexceptional on its own and lacking the charm of its two predecessors. The need for public accomodation had long been admitted; the old Market Hall was grossly inadequate, despite a remodelling in 1866, when accomodation for 300 was provided, along with a platform and 22 large gas lights. Thame acquired two spikey Gothic dissenting chapels during the 1880s, but somehow they do not seem incongruous in the wide expanse of Upper High Street.

Thame is fortunate at present to have few, if any derelict buildings. However, if it did, it might be easier to appreciate better what the town was really like a century ago. Buildings lapsed into a state of not-so-gentle decay; the streets were fairly dirty and ill-drained. Appalling odours pervaded the town from the fell-mongers' yards and the open drains, such as they were. Poverty and ignorance may not have stalked the streets, but they were certainly never far off.

126

We can gain some impression of this society by thumbing through the back numbers of the *Thame Gazette*, which started publication in 1856. The first edition, of 11 March of that year, contained a brief summary of local news on the front page, but like most provincial newspapers of the day, was mostly given over to digests of national news and advertisements for patent medicines and local tradesman. Upwards of 800 copies were printed weekly by 1865, and pride of news place often given over to anecdote and gossip. In December 1877, for example, it reported that a proverbial bull had run into a Mr Jarvis's shop in the Upper High Street, getting as far as the sitting room door. Agricultural, religious and civic matters predominated in the newspaper, and despite the coverage of national and foreign news, one gets an impression of insularity. Government legislation occasionally impinges upon the community, such as when Board Schools have to be established in the 1870s. Yet there is little sense of national pulse, even after the railway had put London only three hours away, and postal services had linked Thame with Australia and Canada.

So Thame a century ago was steeped in and bound by traditions and local issues. The set-up was remarkably feudal, with due deference being paid to the Earl of Abingdon, still a major landowner in the town. The Dowager Lady Wenman of Thame Park, too, achieved a form of aristocratic deference through her generous but eccentric ways. Even the machinations of local government reform failed to change the basic fabric of this society very much. Many of the real changes belong to this century, and the final chapter in this story.

The old post office in High Street.

High Street, as photographed by Taunt in the 1880s. The Market House is in use as a chapel, and there are houses where Nelson Street branches off.

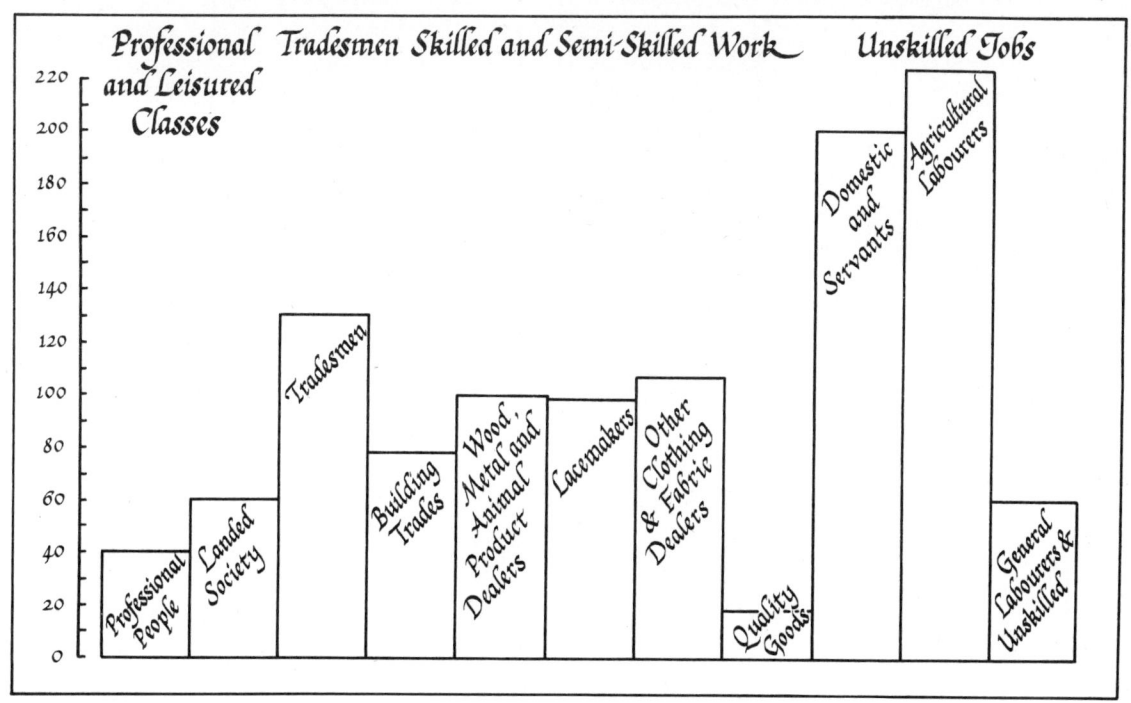

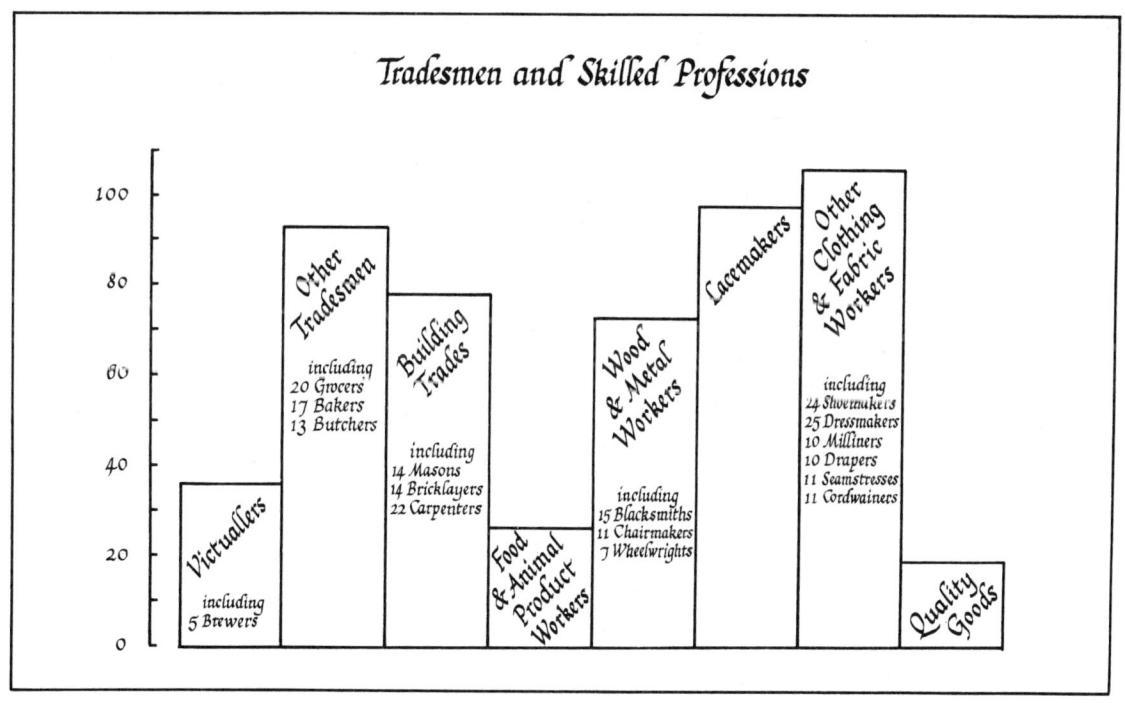

ABOVE: Occupations of the residents of Thame in 1851, according to the census. Paupers, housewives and children are omitted. BELOW: A more detailed analysis of artisans and tradesmen.

1

A page from the 1851 census. The tickets and crossings out were made by the enumerators when checking; an alteration has been made at the bottom.

ABOVE: The South Oxfordshire Hunt meeting in Thame. (QPS) LEFT:
Watch mechanism by William Stone of Thame. (Ash. M) RIGHT: Wills'
tobacconists, by the Town Hall. The shop remains, though changed
in name.

ABOVE: Mellett's, saddlers in High Street. An incredible assortment of wares on display. BELOW LEFT: The old brick kiln in Park Street (formerly Brick Kiln Lane) being demolished. RIGHT: Bandstand in the grounds of the former Grammar School.

Upper High Street, Thame

ABOVE: Shops in Cornmarket. BELOW: Upper High Street,
showing Whitehound pond on the left.

ABOVE: The Institute being opened, 1910. BELOW: The Recreation
field: from an Oxford County School prospectus, and INSET: James Figg,
the prizefighter from Thame.

ABOVE: Cornmarket as it was in about 1876. CENTRE: The Red Lion in Cornmarket as it used to be, (QPS) and BELOW: Cornmarket in about 1920.

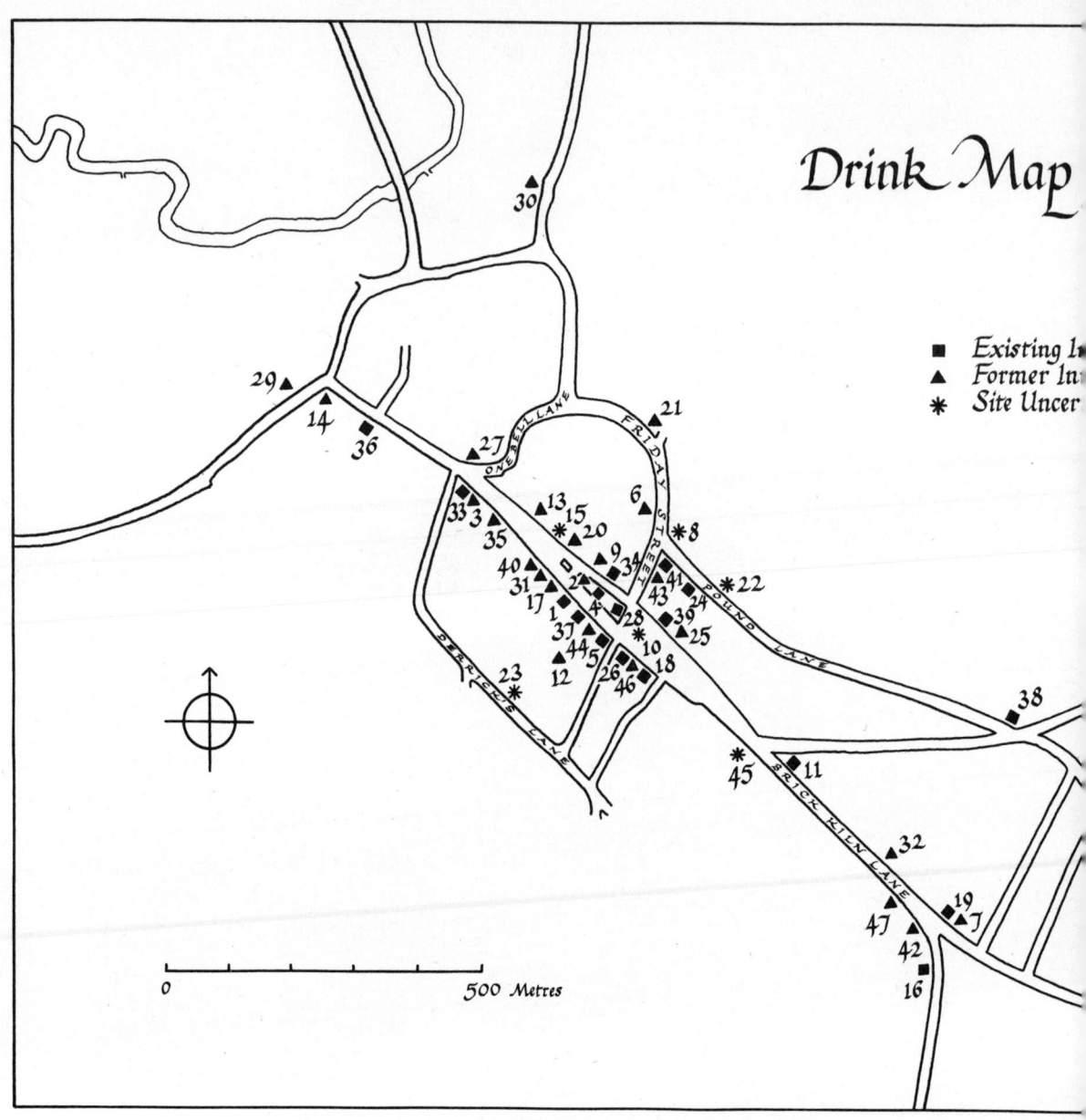

Drink Map

■ Existing I...
▲ Former In...
✳ Site Uncer...

0   500 Metres

ABOVE: The One Bell Inn. LEFT: A pub map of Thame — the list is not exhaustive. Other pubs are known to have existed but their precise locations cannot be ascertained.

KEY: 1. Abingdon Arms (Chequers before 1825) 2. Anchor 3. Arnott's Ale House 4. Birdcage 5. Black Horse (Fleur de Lys in 1838) 6. Old Blue Man (delicensed 1906) 7. Bricklayers Arms 8. Brittania 9. Bull 10. Chequers Ale House 11. Cross Keys 12. Crown (behind Spread Eagle) 13. Crown (burned 1856) 14. Crown (lost licence 1941) 15. Edden's Beer Shop 16. Falcon 17. Fighting Cocks 18. Fox (site formerly occupied by the Angel) 19. Four Horseshoes (formerly Three Horseshoes) 20. Greyhound 21. Greyhound (lost licence 1915) 22. Half Moon (lost licence 1914) 23. Hole in The Wall 24. Jolly Sailor 25. King's Alehouse 26. Nag's Head 27. One Bell Inn (lost licence 1915) 28. Oxford Arms 29. Plough (lost licence 1915) 30. Red Cow (lost licence 1915) 31. Red Lion 32. Red Lion Alehouse 33. Rising Sun 34. Saracen's Head 35. Seven Stars (lost licence 1898) 36. Six Bells 37. Spread Eagle (formerly the Oxford Arms) 38. Star and Garter 39. Swan 40. Taplin's Inn 41. Two Brewers 42. Wenman Arms 43. Wheatsheaf 44. White Horse (lost licence 1910) 45. Whitehound 46. Wood's Alehouse 47. Woolpack (lost licence 1907).

ABOVE LEFT: The Red Cow, Aylesbury Road. RIGHT: The Cross Keys. CENTRE LEFT: the Crown Inn, Priestend. RIGHT: The Greyhound Inn, where Hampden died. BELOW LEFT: Another Greyhound Inn, in North Street. RIGHT: The Six Bells as it was 70 years ago.

ABOVE LEFT: The Four Horseshoes, or Railway Hotel. RIGHT: One Bell Lane, named after the pub, which is just out of view. Now called Bell Lane, and considerably widened. CENTRE: The old Fire Engine House, near Whitehound Pond. RIGHT: The Court House, and BELOW LEFT: many prosperous tradesmen issued their own Trade Tokens in the 17th century.

ABOVE: A view towards Buttermarket, dating from the 1880s. BELOW: A view back down the other way. The area was completely cobbled.

ABOVE: Procession from the King Edward VI memorial service. BELOW:
A living memorial — Thame remembers its dead, and INSET: issue of
Newspaper by the Oxfordshire Yeomanry in 1907.

ABOVE: Election fever in 1910, outside the former post office. CENTRE: Upper High Street in 1911. A bonfire was erected to celebrate the Coronation. BELOW: A busy day in the Cornmarket, about 1900.

In connection with the Coronation Festivities, the COMMITTEE beg to announce that the

DINNER WILL TAKE PLACE

On the Recreation Ground, on

Thursday Afternoon,

AT 5 O'CLOCK,

AND A

Service in the Parish Church,

AT 7 P.M.

There will be NO ALTERATION in the arrangements already made for the

Tea for the Children and Adults,

On FRIDAY.

All other forms of Entertainment have been cancelled, and the Inhabitants are requested NOT TO DECORATE OR ILLUMINATE.

PRINTED BY MEARS & SONS, THAME,

Poster giving details of the Coronation festivities in 1911.

The Thame Gazette

AND OXFORDSHIRE AND BUCKS ADVERTISER.

ESTABLISHED 1856.

VOL. LI.—No. 2,638 {Registered for Transmission in the United Kingdom}   TUESDAY, NOVEMBER 6, 1906.   ONE PENNY (Post Free, 1s. 9d. per Quarter, in Advance.)

Sales by Auction.

By Messrs. BOND & BURROWS.

THAME MARKET.

Messrs. BOND & BURROWS HOLD A SALE OF

FAT & STORE STOCK

In this Market every Tuesday.

Consignments will be esteemed a favour.

By order of the Mortgagee.

SPRIGGS ALLEY, CHINNOR, OXON.

About One mile from Chinnor Station, G.W.R

Messrs. BOND & BURROWS

ARE instructed to SELL by AUCTION, at the ROYAL OAK, CHINNOR, on WEDNESDAY, November 21st, 1906, at 5 o'clock in the Evening, a detached

FREEHOLD COTTAGE,

GARDEN & PADDOCK, together about HALF-AN-ACRE, in the occupation of Mr. Harry Hunt.

The Brick and Stone, Thatched and Slated Cottage contains 3 Bedrooms, Kitchen, Scullery, Pantry, and Lean-to Wood Shed.

Further particulars of William Parker, Esq., Solicitor, Thame, or of the Auctioneers, Thame.

ANNUAL SALE OF FAT STOCK

HOME FARM, WADDESDON, BUCKS, Within a mile of Waddesdon Manor Station, and about 5 from Aylesbury.

Messrs. BOND & BURROWS

ARE favoured with instructions from Miss Alice de Rothschild, to SELL by AUCTION, on the PREMISES, on THURSDAY, November 22nd, 1906, at One o'clock.

76 GRAND FAT CATTLE,
142 FAT DOWN EWES & TEGS,
3 YOUNG PEDIGREE SHORTHORN BULLS.

Further particulars in future advertisements.

Auction and Estate Agents, Thame, Oxon.

By Messrs. FRANKLIN & JONES.

THAME MARKET.

Messrs. FRANKLIN & JONES ATTEND THIS MARKET EVERY TUESDAY, for the SALE by AUCTION of FAT and STORE STOCK.

Auction Offices:—2, Frewin Court, Oxford ; and on Market and Fair Days, at 14, UPPER HIGH STREET, Thame.

SALE THIS DAY.

THAME MARKET.

TUESDAY, NOVEMBER 6th.

INCLUDED in this SALE will be a capital two-year-old CART FILLY, rising 3 years, the property of Mrs. Crook and Son, North Weston.

FRANKLIN & JONES,
Auctioneers,
Oxford and Thame.

OXFORD CATTLE MARKET

WEDNESDAY, NOVEMBER 14th, 1906.

Messrs. FRANKLIN & JONES

WILL hold their usual important SALE by AUCTION of FAT and STORE STOCK, as above.

Numerous entries are already to hand ; early intimation of others will much oblige.

Frewin Court, Oxford.

FORTHCOMING ANNUAL SALES

OF UNDERWOOD

To be held by

Messrs. FRANKLIN & JONES

MONDAY, NOVEMBER 19.—Waterperry Wood, Oxon, by direction of J. J. Henley, Esq., C.B.

THURSDAY, NOVEMBER 22.—Holton Park Estate, Oxon, by direction of H. S. T. Biscoe, Esq.

MONDAY, NOVEMBER 26.—Shabbington and Oakley Woods, Bucks, by direction of J. J Henley, Esq., C.B.

Full particulars later.

Estate Agency Offices, Frewin Court, Oxford.

By Messrs. PAXTON & HOLIDAY.

BEECH TIMBER SALE FIXTURES

AT STOKENCHURCH,

On WEDNESDAY, NOVEMBER 21st, 1906, about

1,000 LOADS OF BEECH,

And a Quantity of OAK and ELM in the following Estates, viz. :

KINGSTON BLOUNT ESTATE, the property of H. C. Brown, Esq.

GURDEN ESTATE, the property of J. C. Brown Esq.

CHINNOR ESTATE, the property of W. A Wykeham-Musgrave, Esq.

AT HIGH WYCOMBE.

On TUESDAY, DECEMBER 4th, 1906.

The annual fall of BEECH, ASH, and OAK, on the WEST WYCOMBE ESTATE, by direction of Sir Robert Dashwood, Bart.

PAXTON & HOLIDAY,
Auctioneers and Estate Agents, Bicester.

. SUMMER REQUISITES. .

EFFERVESING SALINE—Refreshing and Healthgiving

CORN PAINT—Removes without pain the most obstinate Corn.

ANTISEPTIC FOOT POWDER—Most useful for tender Feet.

SKIN SOAP—Excellent for toilet use.

Dr. PEARCE'S HAIR PRODUCER—Is an excellent Hair Tonic.

SANITARY DISINFECTING FLUID & CARBOLIC DISINFECTING POWDER—As Germ destroyers these two preparations have no Superiors, and are most economical to use.

All the above are packed in convenient quantities to suit all requirements, and are Sold only by

R. COLEY, CHEMIST, THAME.

TAILORING

FOR

LADIES & GENTS.

Stylish and Reliable.

NEW SEASON'S CLOTH.

HARRY ROSE,
86, HIGH STREET, THAME.

W. A. WELLS.

ENGLISH & FOREIGN TIMBER MERCHANT

THE SAW MILLS, THAME.

Deals, Battens, Boards, Matching, Weather-boards, Flooring Mouldings, Elm and Oak Boards, and Planks, Oak Posts, and Scantlings.

BROSELEY AND READING TILES,

STAFFORDSHIRE BRICKS AND PIPES

SUPERIOR LIME ALWAYS IN STOCK.

Large Stock of PORTLAND CEMENT from the Associated Portland Cement Manufacturers (1900), Limited.

LORD WILLIAMS'S GRAMMAR SCHOOL, THAME.

SCHOOL RE-OPENED ON TUESDAY, 18th SEPT., 1906.

Important Improvements in Equipment are being made during the vacation in the Lecture Rooms, &c., in readiness for the coming Term.

During the last four years 98 Certificates have been gained in the Oxford Local Examinations, including 30 Honours, and several Distinctions.

Foundation Scholarships are awarded after Examination in May.

Rev. A. E. SHAW, M.A., Oxon, B.Lit., London, Headmaster.

WE WOULD DRAW YOUR ATTENTION -
TO A FEW SPECIAL LINES -

FOR THE COMING SEASON.

GRAND VALUE IN LADIES' JACKETS.

NEW CLOTHS.   NEW SHAPES.

LATEST STYLES IN MILLINERY.

BEST VALUE IN DRESS GOODS.

LADIES' HOSIERY & UNDERWEAR.

WHICH CAN BE OBTAINED AT

WAKEFIELD'S,

108, HIGH STREET, THAME.

Opposite the TOWN HALL.

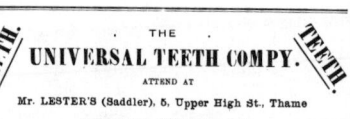

THE

UNIVERSAL TEETH COMPY.

ATTEND AT

Mr. LESTER'S (Saddler), 5, Upper High St., Thame

EVERY TUESDAY,

HOURS — 11.30 till 4.30 (or later by appointment).

PUNCTUAL AND REGULAR ATTENDANCE.

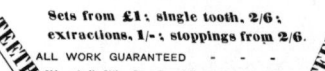

Sets from £1 : single tooth, 2/6 ;
extractions, 1/- : stoppings from 2/6.

ALL WORK GUARANTEED

Old or badly-fitting Cases Remodelled at Moderate Charges.

GENUINE HAND-SEWN BOOTS

FOR

FARM AND GENERAL COUNTRY HARDWEAR.

We MAKE to MEASURE on the New Method Principle, ensuring PERFECT FIT.

OUR MATERIALS ARE THE BEST OBTAINABLE.

OUR PRICES ARE MODERATE.

EVERY PAIR GUARANTEED ABSOLUTELY.

NOTE ADDRESS:—

INTERNATIONAL SHOE CO.,

BESPOKE BOOT MAKERS,
103, HIGH STREET, THAME.

THAME CYCLE & MOTOR DEPOT.

WEST'S

ANNUAL CLEARANCE SALE

COMMENCES

TUESDAY, OCTOBER 23rd, 1906.

The whole of the STOCK of
NEW & SECOND-HAND BICYCLES

Will be offered at exceedingly low prices to clear, in view of alterations to Premises

This Sale is recognised as the best means of obtaining a good sound Machine at a wonderfully low figure.

New and Up-to-date Bicycles by the best Manufacturers, will be offered at great reductions off the lowest cash prices.

It will pay you to purchase now, if you do not want a Machine until next Spring.

MOTOR CARS ON HIRE at SHORT NOTICE & ON REASONABLE TERMS.

NOTED HOUSE FOR RELIABLE MACHINES.

Miscellaneous.

Mr. C H. COLLINS, A.R.C.O. BEGS to announce that he Visits THAME, and has Vacancies for PUPILS for PIANO-FORTE, ORGAN, and SINGING.

Address—
Hill View, Roberts Road, High Wycombe.

£10 to £5000 ADVANCED
ON NOTE OF HAND ALONE.

NO calls for Sale taken, or charges made unless business eventuates. Don't apply to so-called Banks or Limited Companies which are registered to conceal the identity of the proprietors or shareholders. I conduct business in my own name and am the actual lender. Write, in confidence, stating requirements, when representative will wait upon you by appointment and complete transaction.

C. WELLS, Corridor Chambers, Leicester

To Hotel Proprietors and Licensed Victuallers.

SILVER HEYDON,

HOTEL & PUBLIC-HOUSE VALUER,
Bell Hotel, Aylesbury, and
Orendon Street, High Wycombe.

ATTENDS THE BLACK HORSE HOTEL, THAME, on TUESDAYS. Persons desirous of disposing of their Business, or requiring Hotels or Public-houses, should apply as above. No sale, no charge. Several Houses to let in this neighbourhood.

TRY
BAILEY'S
SAUSAGES.

FRESH EVERY DAY.

GEORGE BAILEY,

Grocer and Bacon Curer,
107, HIGH STREET, THAME.

MONEY.

THE OLD-ESTABLISHED PROVINCIAL UNION BANK continues to lend immense sums daily, from £15 to £5,000, on Note of Hand alone, or other Security, at a few hours' notice, to all classes in any part of England and Wales, repayable by easy instalments. No good application is ever refused. All communications strictly private. Moderate Interest. Special rates for short periods. The largest, best known, and most honourably conducted Business in the Kingdom. Thousands of our regular customers have expressed their entire satisfaction in repeated transactions with us. If desired, one of our Officials will attend at your residence at once with Cash, and carry out the advance THERE & THEN. Call, or write (in confidence,) to the

MANAGER,
Mr. STANLEY DOWDING,
1, QUEEN SQUARE, BRISTOL.

A SAFE REMEDY

FOR ALL

SKIN & BLOOD DISEASES

If you are suffering from any disease due to an impure state of the blood, such as ECZEMA, SCROFULA, SCURVY, BAD LEGS, BLOOD POISON, GLANDULAR SWELLINGS, ABSCESSES, SORES, BOILS, PIMPLES, RHEUMATISM, GOUT, &c., you should take the value of Clarke's Blood Mixture, the world-famed Blood Purifier and Restorer. It is warranted to cleanse the blood from all impure matter from whatever cause arising.

Thousands of testimonials from all parts of the world. A recent case is given below:—

LASTING CURE OF ECZEMA.

Mr. JAMES PITTMAN, of Woolston borough, near Dover, writes:—"You will recollect my sending to you for six bottles of 'Clarke's Blood Mixture' a year ago or more. Well, I am glad to say that I am now quite restored and free from Eczema. I think it must be for ten years that I suffered from it. I was under a doctor for several years, but did not derive much benefit. I ever I find a sufferer I shall always recommend 'Clarke's Blood Mixture.' I should have written to you before, only having had Eczema so badly, I thought it would surely break out again, but I am glad to state that it is quite gone."

CLARKE'S BLOOD MIXTURE

THE WORLD-FAMED BLOOD PURIFIER.

Can be obtained of all Chemists and Stores, 2 9 per bottle, and in Cases containing six times the quantity, 11/-.

BEWARE OF IMITATIONS.

BLANCHARD'S FOR LADIES Supersede Pennyroyal, &c Pil Cochia and Bitter Apple.

APIOL & STEEL PILLS

Recommended for Irregularities In removing all obstructions and relieving the distressing symptoms so prevalent with the sex.

LESLIE MARTYN, LIMITED, LONDON.

CLARKE'S B 41 PILLS are warranted to cure in either sex, all acquired or constitutional Discharges from the Urinary Organs, Gravel and Pains in the back. Free from Mercury. Established upwards of 30 years. In boxes 4s. 6d. each, of all Chemists and Patent Medicine Vendors throughout the World, or sent for sixty stamps by the makers. The Lincoln and Midland Counties Drug Company, Lincoln

---

Front page of the *Thame Gazette,* 6 November 1906. Advertisements did not disappear from the front page until 1965.

ABOVE: The High Street, with the Institute on the right. CENTRE:
North Street: a turn-of-the-century view. BELOW: Fading fast: a sign in
Buttermarket, long since in abeyance.

145

ABOVE: A bleak and muddy scene around the Town Hall in the late 1870s. CENTRE: A view towards the Town Hall in 1904. The Market is taking place in Cornmarket. BELOW: A deserted High Street in the 1880s.

TOWN HALL, THAME.

THIS Hall was built to commemorate the Fiftieth Year of the Reign of Her Most Gracious Majesty Queen Victoria.

The following gentlemen were appointed to form a Building Committee, by whose direction this Hall was erected, and handed over to the Thame Local Board.

Chairman—PHILIP J. D. WYKEHAM, Esq.

W. A. Wykeham-Musgrave, Esq.
Hon. F. L. Bertie.
Rev. E. B. Corbett.
Rev. W. Morley.
Dr. H. G. Lee.
Messrs. S. Lacey.
" J. W. Marsh.
" J. J. Shrimpton.
" J. S. Stevens.

Messrs. W. Parker.
" J. L. Castle.
" J. Walker.
" P. H. Pearce.
" F. Hawkins.
" J. E. Loosley.
" H. H. Smith.
" C. F. Howland.
" H. T. Mears.
" A. Deverell.

Mr. G. Talbot. *Hon. Secretary and Treasurer.*

THIS Hall was opened on Monday, April 2nd, 1888, and stands upon the site of the old Market Hall. The building is of pressed red brick. The windows and doors are faced with Bath stone. It it 62 feet in height to the top of the spire. The upper windows are gothic-elliptical. The interior consists—on the basement, of three rooms, one of which is used as a reading room, one for a library and bagatelle room, both of which measure 25 feet by 16 feet; and a Council Room, which measures 32 feet by 24 feet. The Hall is approached by a staircase of Portland stone, the ceiling is elliptical and panelled, is 60 feet long by 32 feet wide; it contains a gallery 32 feet by 12 feet. The Hall will seat about 100 persons. The clock in the tower was presented by Samuel Lacey, Esq., and is the work of Messrs. Gillett and Co., Croydon. H. J. Tollit, Esq., of Oxford, was the architect, and Mr. John Wells, of Thame, the builder.

LIST OF SUBSCRIBERS.

ABOVE: From the subscription list for the New Town Hall in 1888.
BELOW: Stribblehills as it was in Lee's time.

147

ABOVE: Modern Thame: problems with traffic. BELOW: Industrial
complexes: the Shell-Mex terminal. (GA)

Changing Thame

This century, Thame has seen changes as wide-ranging as anything that has happened during the previous 600 years. Change has become an accepted characteristic of society, and Thame has not been immune from the process.

The shape of High Street has fortunately been largely preserved, the only major loss being the Girls' Grammar School, demolished in 1965. The whole centre is now a conservation area, and the Local Draft Plan (1978) envisages no substantial alterations, though controversy may well rage over intended restrictions on traffic and parking. The main proposals include moderate development of the site mentioned above, between High Street and Southern Road, and a new Police Station in Bell Lane/North Street, some re-adjustment of the cattlemarket, and a small residential development in Wellington Street.

Although considerable emphasis is now being placed on conserving the 'character' of the High Street, in one respect there has been a substantial and probably irreversible change taking place gradually in this century. Far fewer family businesses exist today, and many of the shops are in the hands of multiple chains. Even the local newspapers are printed and published outside the town. Comparison with an old directory at the turn of the century will reveal how few old-established firms have survived unscathed to the present day.

Thame's major developments recently have been outside the traditional centre. Several new estates were begun after the last war, including building on the old Barley Hill field, and the largest development, Lea Park Estate, is still proceeding. Part of the access road will eventually form a link around the town. Meanwhile, Thame still waits for work on its by-pass to begin, first proposed back in the 1930s. Although a lot of the congestion on the A418 is due to through traffic, the town generates a lot of traffic as a shopping centre, and several new industries have expanded road traffic fleets. The large Shell BP depot near the old railway station opened in 1958, and along the adjacent Wenman Road are several new developments through a wide range of industries providing diverse employment for the area.

Increased reliance now has to be placed upon the motor car. The nearest railway link is now Princes Risborough—but no regular buses go there. The nearness of the M40 has, however, brought a recent increase in commuting to High Wycombe and London. According to the 1971 census, 68.2% of families in Thame owned one or

149

more cars, and 44.4% of residents worked outside Thame. 31.3% of the local work force were in skilled manual occupations, whilst only 2.8% were actively engaged in working on the land—a sharp reversal compared with 100 years ago! The average Thame family in 1978 would be in their 30s with two children, in blue-collar employment, owning a house of five rooms, and commuting by car to Oxford or High Wycombe daily.

Projections for population growth suggest that Thame's figure of 7,500 in 1978 could rise to about 11,500 in the 1980s, mostly through completion of the Lea Park Estate. No other major development is planned at present. However, the expansion has not been without birth-pangs. Local schools have had to become used to seemingly endless expansion. Some new facilities, like the Health Centre, have sometimes resulted. However, Thame lacks many of the facilities enjoyed by neighbouring towns of similar size, like indoor sports facilities, heated swimming pools, or public halls, theatres or cinemas. The Thame Players did acquire the former Church Hall in Nelson Street in 1977, but venues for concerts and performances are still limited.

However, this has not inhibited the citizens of Thame from enjoying their leisure time. The Town Guide of 1977 lists no less than 60 active societies, ranging from political clubs and sporting associations to social groups, resident's associations and even a Historical Society. A Youth Centre caters for the young whilst the elderly have benefited from purpose-built accommodation such as Meadowcroft. Sports flourish locally. On the negative side, so does vandalism. Thame has had to adapt to the problems as well as the privileges of modern life.

Yet Thame still has a distinct character which emerges on the 'big' occasions. The September show and fair are amongst the largest and most impressive in this part of the country. In recent years, Thame has branched out into regular Carnivals, a rag week (run by the students of Rycotewood College), and an annual entry in the 'Britain in Bloom' competition. Though nowadays somewhat submerged by the large embrace of South Oxfordshire District Council, the town still boasts a Mayor and Council. In 1977, Thame was linked with the French town of Nontron, near Bourdeaux.

'The Thame community have not led the van in any new crusade, or manned the last stronghold of a dying cause; rather they have remained spectators of the national scene.' So concluded Brown and Guest, in the last (and first!) full-scale history of the town, published in 1935. Yet Thame itself does represent a kaleidoscope of changing fashions, opinions, loyalties, sufferings and pleasures. Though the main stream of history has not often diverted its flow into the town, that does not mean that it's past is irrelevant, or without interest. Thame's future indeed lies closely linked to its past, preserving the best of what remains, and moulding the town to the needs of the 20th century. Floreat Thamensis!

New industries: Angus Fire Armour.

A supermarket plugs the gap left by the demolition of the former Girls' Grammar School. INSET: William Guest: the last historian to write on Thame.

Bibliography

Standard Works:
Lupton. History of Thame and its Hamlets
Lee. History and Antiquities of the Prebendal Church of St.
Mary's, Thame
Brown and Guest. A History of Thame. 1935
Victoria County History of Oxfordshire, Volume 6. 1962
Other General Works:
Emery. The Oxfordshire Landscape, 1974
Sherwood and Pevsner. The Buildings of England,
Oxfordshire. 1974
Rogers. This was their world. 1973
Specific Works:
(a) *Books*
J. H. Brown. A short History of Thame School
J. Fothergill. Diary of an Innkeeper
N. O'Connor. Goddes Peace and the Queenes
A. Wood. Diaries
(b) *Pamphlets and other sources:*
A. J. Baines. The Baptists of Thame
B. Bunford. The Enclosures of Thame and Otmoor.
(Typescript, OCRO)
HMSO. Rycote Chapel
C. Morris. The Rycote Yew
G. Parsons. The Inns of Thame
St Mary's Church. Official Guide
South Oxfordshire District Council, Thame Draft Plan, 1978
Thame Official Town Guides
In addition, there are numerous Directories of the area, and
newspapers such as *Jackson's Oxford Journal* (covering the
18th and 19th centuries) and *The Thame Gazette* (from 1865),
give good coverage.
The Mediaeval Churchwardens' Accounts have been published
intermittently in the Journals of the Berks, Bucks and Oxon
Record Society.
Several of the publications of the Oxfordshire Record Society
deal with Thame matters, as does the Journal *Oxoniensia*.

KEY TO CAPTION CREDITS

Ash.M	Ashmolean Museum, Oxford
AM	Aylesbury Museum
BL	Bodleian Library, Oxford
OMS	Oxfordshire Museum Services, Woodstock
OCRO	Oxfordshire County Record Office
PRO	Public Record Office
GA	Gannet Air, Thame (N. S. Lilley)
QPS	Queensway Photographic Services (N. S. Lilley)
MN	Michael Newitt
RM	Ron Mott
WM	W. Mackenzie

Index

154

Subscribers

Presentation copies

1 Thame Council
2 Oxfordshire County Council
3 Thame Library
4 Cllr Len Webb
5 Peter Kingham
6 William Owen Hassall
7 Frank Jessup

8 Gerald Clarke
9 Clive Birch
10 Mrs J. P. Bailey
11 P. A. Shewry
12 A. D. Lewis
13 Miss J. M. Peters
14 G. R. Southern
15 Mrs H. M. Dicker
16 Mrs G. Hurst
17 Mrs B. Capstick
18 J. Pearson
19 Mrs A. H. Thomas
20 G. A. Poulter
21 Mrs V. E. Reynolds
22 Mrs O. L. Bishop
23 Mrs C. P. Smith
24 B. H. Wood
25 W. G. Elsey
26 Mrs Fleming
27 Mrs H. Bracegirdle
28 Mrs J. Williams
29 Mrs S. P. Phillips
30 M. Kirtland
31 Mrs C. Thomas
32 Mrs Ann Hooton
33 W. L. Matthews
34 Mrs M. Beeney
35 Mrs A. Cockburn
36 Peter Chard
37 A. Patchett
38 Bob and Jill Mitchell
39 N. G. Waters
40 V. Wallis
41 Mrs Jane Napier
42 Mrs D. Slay
43 J. Hetherington
44 V. Stevens
45 P. L. Dudley
46 Mrs M. R. Carr
47 T. M. & D. W. Timms
48 Mr & Mrs P. R. Palfrey
49 W. T. Gillard
50 P. A. Gillard
51 Ronald D. Cherrington
52 Michael J. Reading
53 Mrs J. Silver
54 Mrs N. Sargant
55 C. J. Wilkinson
56 Mrs M. S. Moss
57 J. R. Cox
58 A. K. Potter
59 Mrs A. Quainton
60 C. Miniati
61 J. A. Lloyd
62 Mrs H. Brennan
63 Mrs M. A. Smith
64 R. A. Kendall
65 Mrs Z. Donald
66 Miss H. M. Hamilton
67 Mrs E. M. Smith
68 Marion Carter
69 A. Hawkes
70 Mrs P. Fowler
71 G. A. Watkins
72 Mrs F. M. Balch
73 Mrs J. Munday
74 Mrs J. Mayl
75 R. E. Mott
76 Mrs J. R. Thompson

77 B. S. Parcell
78 D. H. Clifton
79 D. R. Barker
80 Mrs M. Fryer
81 Mrs I. G. Brand
82 Miss A. Aldridge
83 Mrs V. Aldridge
84 P. Hawkins
85 Brian Brason
86 J. M. Clarke
87 C. R. Butterfield
88 T. Joyce
89 Miss P. J. Paton
90 R. Richter
91 Mrs P. Collins
92 Mr & Mrs R. Roberts
93 David Paul Stollery
94 Mrs Barbara Waters
95 Miss E. G. Dobson
96 Mrs Molly Day
97 Margaret G. Wood
98 R. F. Lindars
99 R. E. C. Procktor
100 M. M. Clarke
101 H. & J. M. Repton
102 I. Claytor
103 Ian & Jane Crabbe
104 D. T. Ashe
105 Brian R. Young
106 Rodney W. Young
107 J. A. Anderson
108 Mrs J. Abbott
109 K. Chapple
110 T. R. P. Cooke
111 J. W. Crockford
112 Mrs H. Connor
113 R. C. Flippance
114 Mrs K. Fell
115 B. A. Daniels
116 Mrs J. Day
117 John Cahillane
118 Mrs D. C. Smith
119 G. T. Smith
120 M. R. Scowen
121 D. G. Stevens
122 Mrs J. Shrimpton
123 Mrs T. G. Austin
124 C. D. Yates
125
126 Mrs M. H. Smith
127 N. R. Smith
128 Mrs D. E. Slay
129 John S. Sermon
130 P. A. Tucker
131
132 Mrs J. Rogers

133 R. E. Rushbrook
134 Miss G. Read
135 Mrs P. Cullen
136 B. M. Currier
137 Mrs Marjorie Power
138 Carol Ann Flint
139 Mrs J. Clarke
140 F. W. Green
141 David Low
142 Mrs M. E. Airstone
143 B. E. Russell
144 A. V. Ramsey
145 W. O. Ross
146 B. Ward
147 Mrs E. M. Whiteman
148 M. G. Warner
149 E. I. Williams
150 Douglas Henry Shrimpton
151
152 R. P. Woods
153 Mrs T. J. Wilkins
154 Mrs Joy K. Weighell
155 C. K. Wiggs
156 Mrs D. L. Warman
157 D. A. Vickers
158 J. Timms
159 A. J. Turner
160 C. W. Thom
161 K. N. Twynman
162 J. W. Steel-Clarke
163 Oxfordshire County Libraries
164
165 M. E. Partridge
166 The Patey Family
167 Mrs R. Pring-Mill
168 T. Carter
169 S. Peacock
170 Mrs C. M. I. Peck
171 Mrs P. A. Massey
172
173 Mrs J. Pilcher
174 Gareth J. Price
175 G. J. Presland
176 Mrs J. Plater
177 Mrs A. J. Penn
178 J. C. Adams
179 Eileen Louise Atkinson
180 Edward Allmond
181 L. R. Parmenter
182 Mr & Mrs J. Parish
183 N. S. Lilley
184 D. Lilley
185 G. K. Pullen

186 A. Odell
187 Mr & Mrs Ord
188 Barbara Osborne
189 G. E. T. Osborne
190 M. Newitt
191 S. J. Hearn
192 Mrs J. Clarke
193 Mr & Mrs G. S. Nebel
194 Mrs W. Webb
195
196 D. Jackson
197 P. H. Winson
198 R. E. Waite
199 E. Whitaker
200 Mrs J. Woodman
201
202 Stanton Haynes
203 F. A. Wright
204 K. O. Wright
205 Mrs A. E. Wheeler
206 Sylvia Watson
207 Alistair E. C. Haimes
208 Eliot B. A. Haimes
209 F. Warwick
210 Nora Walker
211 R. A. Wilkins
212 Miss C. Nappin
213
214 R. Fleming
215 Mr & Mrs R. Kellenberger
216 Mrs Margaret King
217 Lilian Joyce
218 Mrs P. M. Jones
219 Mrs E. Jackman
220 Mrs A. Jones
221 D. C. Jones
222 J. E. Fulkes
223 Mrs M. D. Fulkes
224 Mrs C. Gascoigne
225 A. Johnson
226 G. B. Hall
227 F. C. Hutt
228 Barri Haynes
229 R. A. Howes
230 R. J. Hardwood
231 Mrs P. P. Heath
232 Miss E. E. Howes
233 Mrs P. Harmes
234 Mrs J. Hurrell
235 A. Houlston
236 Miss M. E. Haslam
237 R. A. Neil
238 G. H. Clarke
241
242 W. G. McKenzie
243 Doris H. Mackereth
244 Miss C. M. Mellers
245 Rev R. E. May
246 Mrs J. Mackay
247 J. K. Michie
248
249 Mrs Mudd
250 Ann Midwinter
251 Mr & Mrs T. F. Mayfield
252 E. K. Maugham
253 R. S. W. Malcolm
254 T. J. Morton
255 A. R. Morgan
256 Jeremy Paul Munro
257 Mrs J. B. R. Marsh

258 Dr A. C. Markus
259 Mrs Patricia Cooper
260 Brian Alan Youens Fleet
261 J. E. Munday
262 E. Lovegrove
263 Mr & Mrs Paul Larkins
264 Mrs S. E. Hotchkiss
265 Mrs Applegarth
266 B. P. Helme
267 Jack Lazenby
268 Mrs C. Lambourne
269 Mrs Nancy Lancaster
270 E. W. Lawrence
271 Mr & Mrs C. H. Simpson
272 Michael G. Smith
273 T. Betteridge
274 M. Pilditch
275 N. Sudron
276 Mrs E. C. Silver
277 D. J. M. Lee
278 The Kirtland Family
279 Christopher Kenyon
280 David H. Kennett
281 Mrs D. Bowles
282
283 The Headley Family
284 Mr & Mrs John Hussey
285 Mrs Julia Hutton
286 Mrs G. E. House
287 M. Hunt
288 Mrs E. Hall
289 R. C. A. Andrews
290
291 Miss R. Horgan
292 Mrs W. Hunter
293 D. J. Hayfield
294 R. Hardiman
295 N. House
296 H. W. Howland
297
299 R. M. Adams
300 J. Grace
301 J. Green
302 Miss Jean Giles
303 Mrs E. J. Fenemore
304 Mrs H. M. Finnerty
305 Mrs E. Beryl K. Flitter
306 I. M. Fulcher
307 F. G. Field
308 J. A. Gibb
309 Mrs R. Griffiths

310 St Andrews School, Oxford
311 Mrs Roslaie F. Gibson
312 R. Groves
313 R. Greenall
314 Mrs N. Hughes
316
317 Mrs C. Franklin
318 Mrs J. Davies
319 Mrs S. Donald
320 D. Dodds
321 R. A. I. Dees
322 Miss Dobinson
323 C. F. Dawson
324 Mrs J. Davies
325 Mrs Leila Davies
326 A. R. Christie-Mutch
327 D. J. W. Cowler
328 Mr & Mrs R. P. Cramp
329 Mrs P. M. Coleman
330 Janette Coleman
331 Mr & Mrs Czemko
332 M. E. Bryant
333 Philip Birtles
334 S. W. Hester
335 MBE FGS
336 Patricia Braithwaite
337 Mrs C. Beamsley
338 F. S. Beedham
339 Mr & Mrs R. W. Bale
340 Mrs Maureen J. Baker
341 Mr & Mrs D. Branch
342 C. Bowler
343 G. Bambrough
344 D. Bradnack
345 Dr A. M. Lambert
346
347 C. R. Butterfield
348 Edgar Astaire
349 J. Brandon
350 Mrs M. Dines
351 Mrs F. C. de Paula
352 R. E. Clark
353 A. J. Clark
354 County Record Office, Aylesbury
355 Miss R. A. E. Bloxham
356 Bodigian & Co Ltd

357 M. J. Beech
358 Werner Braun
359 D. A. J. Barnard
360 Sir Frank
361 Bowden Bt
362 C. A. Burrows
363 Mr & Mrs J. A. Bell
364 Derek Brown
365 J. A. Beattie
366 L. S. Bright
367 Mrs Benning
368 M. J. Ball
369 A. J. Ball
370 C. R. Simpson
371 C. G. Smith
372 A. C. Ritchie
373 Miss L. Rose
374 Dorothy I. Fitch
376
378 F. J. Pearman
379 Mrs M. Brooks
380 G. W. Broom
381 Mrs Burke
382 Mrs P. Rymills
383 Mrs G. M. Briars
384 E. Badger
385 Mrs J. H. Brown
386 Philip Chaplin
387 A. F. Coulson
388 A. Cleaver
389 Mary T. Cadle
390 George Craker
391 P. C. Cox
392 Mrs M. W. Copp
393 John & Roelie Reed
394 Dr D. A. Stormonth
395 R. Shrimpton
396 Mrs W. Soult
397 Mrs D. S. Stone
398 Dr G. Stores
399 Mrs K. Chaulk
400 Mrs R. M. Austin
401 Mrs A. Colwell
402 Mrs R. Crowdy
403 Mrs A. D. Castle
404 Roger D. Collins
405 Mrs J. Miniati
406 Mrs M. C. Upton
407 J. D. Stephenson
408 G. W. Pulling
409 Mrs Quartz
410 Peter Playford
411 A. F. Ireson
412 Miss Juliet McCormick
413 Victoria & Albert Museum

414 Stephen & Vicki Wegg-Prosser
415 Malcolm Read
416 David Read
417 John Walker
418 Joan & Tony Lammiman
419 Mrs E. A. Jeffery
420 Mrs J. Fujak
421 D. G. Stevens
422 Mrs M. H. White
423 N. P. Fleet
424 Mrs Collier
425 Mrs R. C. Jones
426 B. J. Broom
427 Rotary Club of Thame
428 G. Smith
429 C. Austin
430 Mrs D. Lambert
431 A. Blunt
432 Mrs Jennie Howes
433 Mrs B. Johnson
434 Robert Gatward
435 Mrs W. Howland
436 Mrs Ilbery
437 Constance M. Gadge
438 W. Neal
439 L. S. Bright
440 M. J. Neal
441 E. Eeles
442 Raimund and Mrs Katharine M. G. Span
443 Mrs Fewell
444 Mrs Simmonds
445 Miss J. Deverell
446 F. W. Green
447 Mrs Nora E. Avery
448 G. Webb
449 Dr A. S. Beer
450 W. Neal
451 B. J. Hanson
452 R. James
453 John P. Seabrook and Gill Knight
454 Miss M. Murche
455 Mrs M. Tomlyn
456 Mrs E. Jackman
457 W. Honour
458 Arthur Shaw

Remaining names unlisted

ENDPAPERS: FRONT: Thame in 1858 (MN) BACK: Map of Thame 1880.

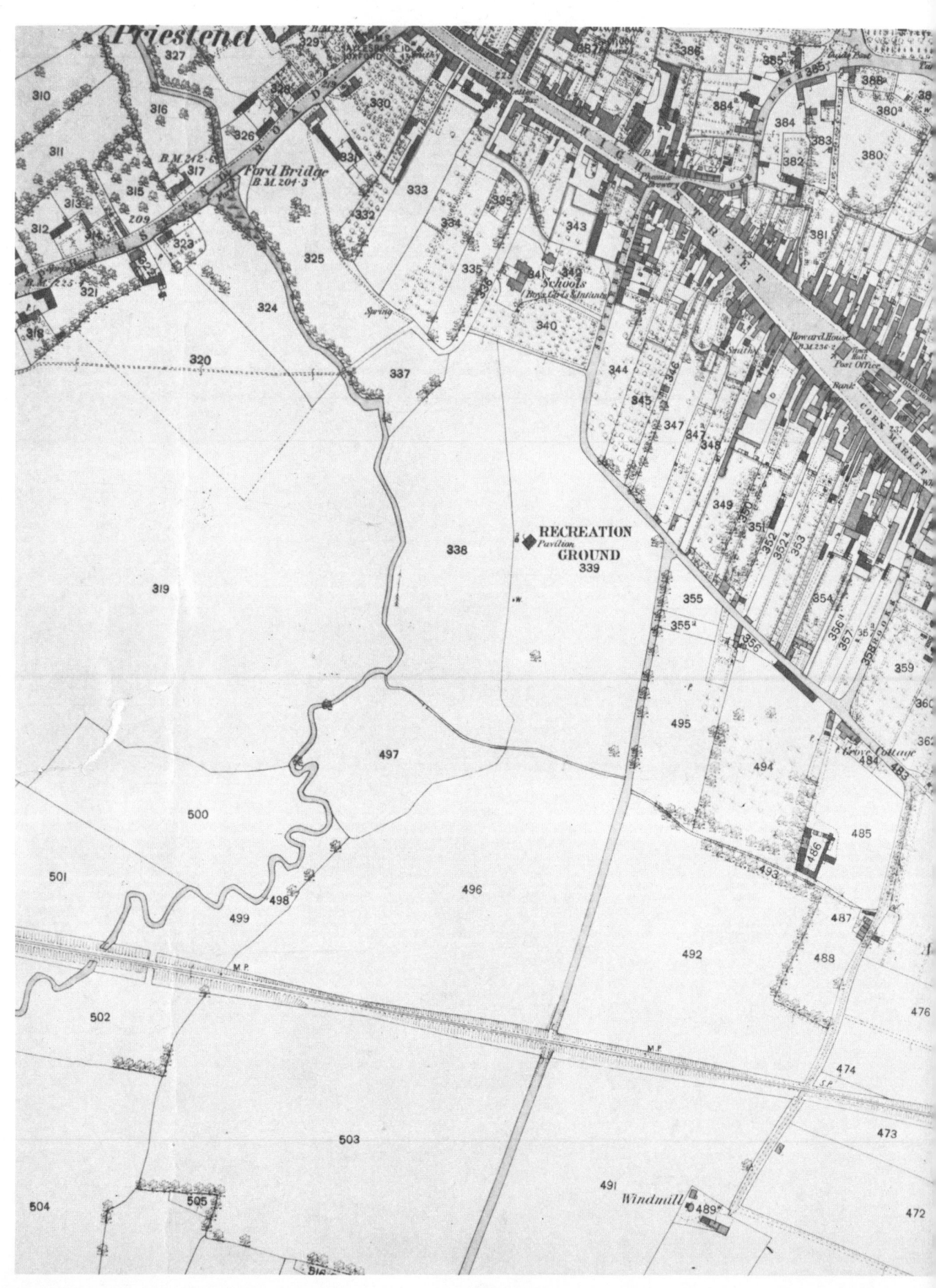